Macedonian C
Learning Stewardship Principl

By

Funsho Oluro

HebrewsFourTwelve Publishing

Printed and published in the United Kingdom.
First Printing, June 2015
Publisher: HebrewsFourTwelve Publishing
Cover design: Midas Creations

ISBN: 978-0-9933091-0-6

Contents

3

Dedication

To Pastor Moses Adekunle Adejola who took me under his wing just after I became a believer in my late teens. He showed me – and still shows – true Christlikeness in word and deed. I will forever be indebted to him for helping to establish me in the faith, and for continuing to encourage me in it.

Acknowledgements

I am deeply indebted to my dear friend, Dr Uche Igbokwe who encouraged my notion of fanning to flame the gift of teaching in me again. It was he who encouraged me to turn a few pages of a blog article into this book. He then patiently read and made useful suggestions about the manuscript several times over the couple of years it took to write it.

I am also really thankful to my beloved brothers, James R. Gray and Simon Fairnington for their help with critiquing the manuscript and their interrogation of my theology of stewardship. Their contributions were particularly useful in clarifying and moderating my thoughts as I wrote in the early stages of this work.

Special thanks also go to my friend Onajomo '*Onas*' Aggreh of Midas creations who kindly helped to design the book cover.

My gratitude also goes to both Phyllis Parish and Seyi Dada who graciously helped with the final editing in preparation for publishing.

I am also thankful to my wife, Linda for her quiet encouragement and for giving me a peaceful home in which I could study and write. I also thank my children, Oreoluwa and Praise for their constant "*Are we there yet*?" queries that spurred me on even when I struggled with focus, strength and motivation.

Last but my no means the least, I give thanks to the triune Father, Son and Spirit for calling me into, and sustaining me in, this dance of cooperation with them in life and ministry.

First Words

Giving is all about Stewardship

As you will probably agree, few subjects produce as much passionate debate in the Christian world today as the subject of giving does. It is unfortunately often narrowed down to financial or material giving alone. It has always been a source of contention since the beginning of the Church till now due to disputes about what and how much faithful Christians should give.

A survey of New Testament scriptures will show even the casual enquirer, that Jesus and the Apostles had an awful lot to say about the relevance of money and material things to practical living in God's kingdom. They often linked the way believers acquired and used material things to how God-pleasing or otherwise their temporal and spiritual lives were. It is therefore important to examine what the Bible in general, and the New Testament in particular, has to say about this important subject.

Through the ages, Christians have constantly wrestled with basic questions like: *'What am I to give?'*, *'How much am I to give?'*, and *'To whom or for what am I to give?'* It is therefore a comfort to know that the scriptures have sufficient guidance in them to help answer these questions. This guidance can help an inquiring disciple of Christ understand practically, what it means to be a free and faithful steward of all the resources with which God blesses him or her. The beauty of this guidance is that it is not just general, but it is also adaptable to individual believers' circumstances. We will hopefully discover these vital truths in our exploration of the various aspects of the guidance available in the scriptures.

The primary objective of this book is therefore to help believers gain a clearer understanding of the main principles of Christian giving by looking at them from the perspective of a steward. This is because, in the final analysis, giving is all about stewardship. We hope to see this clearly throughout the journey of discovery through this study. Faithful stewardship is the *'Master key'* that unlocks the riches of Christ-centred giving. Christians who mainly have only a dutiful or worse still, a *'what's in it for me?'* perspective of giving cannot be faithful stewards of the resources that they hold in trust for God in the long term. Hence, the principles that we will be sharing are founded on a sound understanding of this fundamental truth.

The study that led to the writing of this book was inspired by some robust discussions on Christian giving I participated in a couple of years ago. These discussions took place, both in live fellowship and online forums. They revealed how shockingly little some of us who were expressing strong opinions had actually explored the broad expanse of scriptures to see what they had to say about the topic. Most of the arguments advanced were based on the teachings and practices that were received from leaders rather than on a personal search and application of the scriptures. Some of these teachings and practices were definitely sound and biblically inspired. Some were however unhelpful and misleading *'traditions of men'* that have become fixed doctrinal teachings. This, sadly, was despite the fact that some of these traditions have veered away from God's original intentions revealed in the scriptures. The dogmatic stance that many of us took gives credence to Jack Deere's poignant words*: "Experience and tradition determine the majority of what church people believe, rather than the careful, patient and personal study of the scriptures"*.

It is important to appreciate from the beginning that chapters 8 and 9 of Second Corinthians, which we will be examining in some detail, relate specifically to the raising of a special welfare offering in aid of far-off Christians rather than to regular giving within the local church. Most of the lessons to be learned from it are however broadly applicable to Christian giving and stewardship in general.

It is particularly instructive that in the New Testament's Book of Acts and the Apostolic Letters, a significant number of the references about offerings relate to giving in aid of missionaries and saints that were not part of the local church in which the offerings were being collected. It is therefore reasonable to assume that the apostles who wrote the letters to the churches took it for granted that believers were already supporting their local churches and the needy within them. This was in addition to the believers being actively committed to supporting mission work and believers outside their immediate environment.

It should inspire us present-day Christians that these first-century Christians were *'big picture'* saints who had a circle of concern that spread beyond what God was doing within their immediate geographic vicinity. This is despite the fact that the world they lived in was a much less interlinked global village than the one we are in today. They saw playing an active part in the establishment and growth of the Church beyond their own borders as being worthy of the investment of a considerably amount of their resources. We who live in today's amazingly interconnected world therefore have less excuse for having a *'small picture'* perspective and care for God's global kingdom.

Giving transcends money

Although this book focuses mainly on financial and material giving, it is only a part – though an important one – of the service of stewardship to which God has called us. Christ bought us with His blood to be His very own possession in order for us to serve Him with our entire being: our spirit, soul and body. As scriptures like Mark 12:28-32 shows, we are called to give much more than our money to the service of God's kingdom; we are called to give our all to it.

Unfortunately, too great a number of Christians actually find it more convenient just to turn up regularly – or not so regularly – for weekly services and give money in the form of tithes and offerings as they partake in the worship service. They do not find it needful or convenient to fully commit to serving God and His Church with their time and talents. We must accept that God cannot be bought off from His demand for our full stewardship by the giving of our finances. He demands our full stewardship and not just token offerings and half-hearted service commitments. These may help to calm our religious conscience but they do not truly fulfil His purpose for us and for His kingdom. Hence, the challenge we constantly face is how best to deploy our entire God-given physical, intellectual, emotional and spiritual faculties in the service of His kingdom in a dynamic and balanced way. As we will see later, this challenge transcends what we do within the confines of 'church' as it is often narrowly defined.

All are gifted to serve

We should begin by acknowledging the there is no such thing as *'a Christian that is not gifted'*. Each believer therefore has gifts with which he or she can make positive differences in God's family. These gifts should be deployed in service both within and outside the confines of the local church. Consequently, we should be committed to identifying and profitably deploying our gifts and abilities as Peter states:

> *10 **Each of you should use whatever gift you have received to serve others, as faithful stewards of God's grace in its various forms.** 11 If anyone speaks, they should do so as one who speaks the very words of God. If anyone serves, they should do so with the strength God*

11

*provides, so that in all things God may be praised through
Jesus Christ. To him be the glory and the power for ever
and ever. Amen.*

1 Peter 4:10-11

In light of the above scripture, a local church is poorer if just
one believer is not using his gifts profitably in her service.
This is a sobering thought as only a few members tend to
provide most of the services in the majority of local
assemblies! Some believers are actually of the mentality that
active Christian service is the duty of those who are specially
'called', 'gifted' or *'paid'* to do so. Hence, it is no wonder
someone likened what takes place in most local churches on a
typical worship day to what happens in the football stadium
on a match day. He said: *"22 players badly in need of a rest are
running around the pitch, being watched, praised and criticised by
22,000 fans badly in need of exercise!"* This may sound amusing,
but sadly, even a casual observation of most churches will
show it to be the painful reality for them.

What stewardship means

One of the best definitions of Christian stewardship is the
working definition adopted by the American Episcopal
Church:

> **"Christian stewardship is grateful and responsible
> use of God's gifts in the light of God's purpose as**

revealed in Jesus Christ. Christian stewards, empowered by the Holy Spirit, commit themselves to conscious, purposeful decisions."

From the above definition, it is clear that a Christian steward is a manager of someone else's resources. He is accountable to the owner for how he uses and manages the resources entrusted to him. Furthermore, stewardship is about conscious, purposeful and consistent commitment to the service of the Master rather than token, undisciplined and haphazard involvement in it. As Paul explains in 1 Corinthians 4:1-5, the most important requirement of stewardship is *"that those who have been given a trust must prove faithful"*. Having such a perspective of the resources we 'have' makes us conscious of the fact that all of them are actually given to us on trust from God. Hence, it is to Him that we will have to render an account when we meet Him face to face after our time on earth is finished as Paul states:

> *10 For we must all appear before the judgment seat of Christ, so **that each of us may receive what is due us for the things done while in the body,** whether good or bad. - 2 Corinthians 5:10*

All the things we do 'while in the body' are the practical expressions of the use of all the tangible and intangible resources we had at our disposal while here on earth; our stewardship. We do well to always remember that we owe our very lives to God, not to talk of all the resources we seemingly 'own'. They are actually nothing but gracious entrustments from His hands, all of which we hold for a limited season. David sums this stewardship perspective brilliantly in 1 Chronicles 29:14

> 14 *"But who am I, and who are my people, that we should be able to give as generously as this?* ***Everything comes from you, and we have given you only what comes from your hand.***

Serving is not limited to 'church'.

Just as giving transcends the financial, our duty of stewardship goes beyond what we do within the confines of our local church building. As a matter of fact, a reading of the Acts of the Apostles, which is the historical account of the early Church, shows that majority of the notable ministry and miracles recorded occurred outside the confines of regular church meetings! In sad contrast, many of today's Christians have been brought up to distinguish too sharply between their 'spiritual' and 'secular' lives in both their thinking and in their living. This leads to an unscriptural separation between how such Christians *'do worship'* on Sunday and *'do life'* during the rest of the week. Jesus and all the New Testament writers clearly taught that the way a Christian acts in his family, neighbourhood and the workplace has a significant effect on both his and the Church's witness.

The following examples of the call to stewardship 'outside' the church should hopefully help you see the above statements in proper perspective:

> Peter taught that how Christians relate with and treat their spouses at home, particularly when one of them is not a believer, has a great impact on the Gospel's effectiveness in the life of the unbelieving spouse. It also has an impact on their receiving and retaining personal blessings from God - 1 Peter 3:1-7.

- Paul warned that the way parents treat their children has an impact on whether or not the children grow up into encouraged and enthusiastic Christians themselves - Ephesians 6:4 and Colossians 3:21
- Paul wrote that when Christian workers serve with diligence and honesty at their workplace, they actually make the gospel attractive to non-Christians - Colossians 3:22-24 and Titus 2:9-10.
- Jesus and Peter both taught that the heavenly Father will be glorified when the people of the world see the good works of his followers in the society - Mathew 5:13-16 and 1 Peter 2:12

From the above examples, it is clear that our call to good stewardship is not limited to what we do in church meetings. The real proof of stewardship is how we work out our Christian faith in our homes, neighbourhood, school or workplace. Our lives as stewards should therefore sanctify our secular lives in such a way that people who meet and know us can witness to our God-glorifying conduct (Mathew 6:13-16). This is what demonstrates that we are wholesome believers who can continually making an impact for God in all facets of everyday life.

Learning with the Corinthians

This book is a journey of exploration in which we will seek to learn from Paul's words of encouragement to the Corinthian believers about the welfare offering they had agreed to take as a contribution to the need of the distressed saints in Jerusalem. Lessons are derived from the principles that formed the basis of Paul's appeal and encouragement to the Corinthians. They were a prominent church in the Imperial Roman Province of Achaia. The principles are extracted and discussed in the same order they flowed out of Paul's letter, even though some might argue that the order could have been improved upon. The order becomes less relevant the more you realise that these principles are interlinked and dynamically interacting.

You will likely discover that you are already practising many of these principles if you have been a committed Christian for some time. Taking this journey should nevertheless help you to gain a clearer understanding of the principles you are already practising, as well as help to draw your attention to the ones on which you need to focus on more. Please note that these principles are not being promoted as means of securing personal material prosperity, though heeding them should lead to greater prosperity of the soul and fruitfulness in God's purpose.

It is recommended that you first carefully read chapters 8 and 9 of Second Corinthians 8 , even if you may have done so several times in the past, before embarking on this study journey. This should help you to focus on the plain teaching of the Bible before engaging with this attempt to interpret and apply the scriptures to our stewardship of the Master's resources that are in our care.

The New International Version of the Bible has been quoted for most of the references because it is relatively familiar to most Christians today, easy to read and accurate enough. Certain parts of the scriptures quoted have been boldened for emphasis in order to draw attention to certain crucial phrases that are considered worthy of special attention in the context of the teaching.

In the following chapters, we will be examining ten principles related to Christian giving that should help us to become more faithful stewards of all the material and intangible resources God gives us. Though a separate principle is covered in each distinct chapter, they are not independent but are all related and interlinked – as things are in real life. Please pray that as you engage with them that you will be enabled to become a more balanced, guilt-free and fruitful steward in God's kingdom.

Principle Challenge:

How closely do you relate financial giving in your life to your call to stewardship in all areas of life?

Principle Prayer:

Lord, please open my eyes afresh to see the breadth and depth of your call to serve You as a faithful steward with my whole life. Help me to learn to daily give my all profitably to Your purposes and glory. Amen.

Principle 1

Grace enables love-inspired Christian giving

1 And now, brothers and sisters, we want you to know about the grace that God has given the Macedonian churches. 2 In the midst of a very severe trial, their overflowing joy and their extreme poverty welled up in rich generosity. 3 For I testify that they gave as much as they were able, and even beyond their ability. Entirely on their own, 4 they urgently pleaded with us for the privilege of sharing in this service to the Lord's people. 5 And they exceeded our expectations: They gave themselves first of all to the Lord, and then by the will of God also to us. 6 So we urged Titus, just as he had earlier made a beginning, to bring also to completion this act of grace on your part. 7 But since you excel in everything —in faith, in speech, in knowledge, in complete earnestness and in the love we have kindled in you —see that you also excel in this grace of giving.

2 Corinthians 8:1-7 (NIV)

The grace of giving and generosity

The Macedonian Christians Paul referred to above demonstrate that love enabled by grace is the greatest motivation for Christian giving. They are held up as examples of how God's grace inspires joyful, liberal and

19

sacrificial giving even in the midst of serious poverty and a great trial of affliction. Unusually, their poverty was mixed with an *'overflow of joy'* that made them insist on giving generously to the cause of their destitute brothers in Jerusalem. This they did, not just within, but well beyond their immediate means in the light of their poverty. The wordings of verses 3 and 4 suggest that Paul and his leadership team tried unsuccessfully to restrain them from giving so much because of their own poor circumstances but they would not be stopped. Instead, they *"urgently pleaded"* with Paul and his team to allow them give so generously. By so doing, they selflessly reached out to provide materially for their Jewish brothers and sisters whose spiritual heritage they had come to share. Paul testifies of this unique benevolence in Romans 15: 25-27:

> *25 Now, however, I am on my way to Jerusalem in the service of the Lord's people there. 26 For Macedonia and Achaia were pleased to make a contribution for the poor among the Lord's people in Jerusalem. 27 They were pleased to do it, and indeed they owe it to them. For if the Gentiles have shared in the Jews' spiritual blessings, they owe it to the Jews to share with them their material blessings.*

Generosity in poverty

Although Paul stated that the Macedonian Christians were in the middle of severe trials, which led to "extreme poverty" at the time they gave their offering, he did not categorically state what caused the trials. The fact that these Macedonians believers were poor despite the fact that they lived in what was then a relatively prosperous Roman Province of Macedonia should arouse curiosity. The sobering reality is that they became committed Christ-followers at a time when, and in a place where, making such stand could cost you your liberty, worldly goods and possibly your very life to persecution. This persecution was most likely what led to the severe trials responsible for their poverty. This is attested to by the history of the church recorded in the New Testament. The Macedonian Church, which started at Philippi, was founded by Paul during his second missionary journey. A careful reading of the Acts 16:6 to 17:15 accounts of its starting at Philippi, and its spread to Thessalonica and Berea show that it was one that faced serious persecution from its very beginning.

Paul's testimony about the Thessalonian Church, the second prominent Macedonian Church, also tells the story of a Church born into persecution, but which was growing in spite of it:

> *4 For we know, brothers and sisters loved by God, that he has chosen you, 5 because our gospel came to you not simply with words but also with power, with the Holy Spirit and deep conviction. You know how we lived among you for your sake. 6 You became imitators of us and of the Lord, **for you welcomed the message in the midst of severe suffering***

21

with the joy given by the Holy Spirit. 7 And so you became a model to all the believers in Macedonia and Achaia.

1 Thessalonians 1:4-7

In 1 Thessalonians 2:14-16, Paul later confirmed that they suffered the same acute persecution from their kinsmen as the Jewish Christians initially suffered from theirs in Judea. This intense persecution would have led to the loss of property, livelihood and maybe the lives of some of those precious saints. This shared suffering must have played a significant role in sensitising them to the troubles of their Jewish brothers and sisters. It partly explains their remarkable generosity towards others going through the hardships and deprivations similar to those they were going through themselves.

Why churches and ministries lack

The outflow of generosity from the relatively poor Macedonian believers is a testimony to a simple yet profound truth: the reason why churches and ministries lack the financial ability to do what God commands them to do is often not due to the material poverty of those who should support them. Rather, on the part of leaders, it is largely due to poor teaching and mentoring of the practice of biblical stewardship. It may also be due to a failure to cast vision in a way that stimulates congregational participation without pressure. On the part of those being led, the main reasons are poor commitment to God, selfishness and the narrowness of vision of life as it relates to their participation in God's kingdom. We shall look at these reasons a bit more lately in our journey through this study.

Following a good example

Paul cites the Philippian church as an example of a church committed to faithful giving in difficult circumstances. They were consistent and generous supporters of Paul's apostolic mission as he testifies in Philippians 4:14-16:

> *14 Yet it was good of you to share in my troubles. 15 Moreover, as you Philippians know,* **in the early days of your acquaintance with the gospel, when I set out from Macedonia, not one church shared with me in the matter of giving and receiving, except you only;** *16 for even when I was in Thessalonica,* **you sent me aid more than once when I was in need.**

When Paul wrote the letter to the Corinthians in the early years of the Church, it had not yet split into separate denominations. Individual churches were simply identified by the name of the place in which they were located or the name of the person in whose house they met. The identity of the Macedonians referred to by Paul in this Corinthians text may therefore be narrowed down to the Philippians (Philippians 4:10-19), and maybe the Thessalonians (1

Thessalonians 1:2-10). Their faithful giving and missionary support, which are discussed in some detail in Paul's letter to the Philippians and Thessalonians, give us reasonable grounds to believe this. Other churches in the province of Macedonia like that of Berea may have also participated in contributing to this offering.

Giving's deepest inspiration

The secret of the Macedonians' extreme generosity lay in the fact that they had first given themselves entirely to the Lord in loving consecration. This is always the foundation for true worship and material giving by any believer, whatever the age in which they live. The Macedonians then went further by committing to the support of the true apostolic ministry of Paul and his partners. Their giving was the natural outflow of the radical commitment that led them to regard giving sacrificially to a worthy cause as "service to the Lord's people". This kind of whole-hearted commitment is the same that was shown by many in the first church community in Jerusalem as Acts 4 and 5 records. It was such dedication that facilitated the breakout of healthy fellowship and miraculous outreach of the first church in Jerusalem.

It can thus be seen from the example of the early church community above that the level to which a Christian will give himself and his material possessions consistently to kingdom causes is directly in proportion to how much his heart is truly given over to the Lord first. A Christian who has committed his whole being to following his Saviour in a life of discipleship will more readily give his substance to Christ-honouring causes. A believer who is not so committed is by contrast more likely to not give at all, or at least not give as much as he should. Worse still, he will be more likely motivated to give mainly for selfish reasons; for what he can get back. This reality is probably why John Wesley, the great Methodist preacher, insightfully remarked that *"the last part of a man to get converted is his wallet"*.

It is instructive that the Corinthian church that was situated in the Roman Province of Achaia was relatively at peace. It was also much more materially prosperous than the Macedonian church at the time this offering was being collected. They, fortunately, had not gone through the extreme persecution and the resultant poverty of the Macedonians at that time. This meant they had relatively much more to give to worthy causes. So for the more prosperous Corinthians, the extravagant sacrifice of the much poorer Macedonians was particularly inspirational. As a result, Paul's commendation of the Macedonians' generous giving must have struck a vital chord in their hearts - as it should do in ours.

The 'excelling' church

Paul testified that the Corinthian church did 'excel in everything': in the areas of faith, speech, knowledge, earnestness and love. They were a church that was not just plodding on but were outstanding in many areas of Christian grace and experience despite their spiritual immaturity. He therefore urged them to apply the same spirit of excellence to the 'grace of giving' for this worthy cause. He was in effect saying to them: *"You already have the mentality and grace from God to do really well in this area of material giving on the evidence of how well you are already doing in other important areas"*.

All Christian leaders and parents should find it instructive that Paul was careful to identify the areas where the Corinthian Saints were already doing well and praise them specifically for these. He did this, even as he urged them to improve in the areas where they were lacking. The best teachers and instructors in virtually all areas of human endeavour are usually those who pinpoint and reinforce the strengths of their students while challenging them to improve in their areas of weakness. Paul, the 'Master Teacher' he was, did this time and time again in his letters to the churches, and to individuals like Timothy and Titus.

The Tabernacle building experience

An incident relevant to the Macedonians' extravagant generosity that is recorded in scripture is when the Israelites were begged to stop giving is in Exodus 35:4 to 36:7. Moses had delivered God's instruction to the Jews in the wilderness to bring different kinds of offerings for the building of the Tabernacle. The people were moved in their hearts to give to the Tabernacle project and they responded so willingly and

26

so generously that their continued giving eventually became a hindrance to the actual progress of the project! The builders and artisans responsible for the project had to appeal to the people through Moses to stop bringing gifts so that they could get on with the work as the people had already brought more than enough materials to get the job done.

Needless to say, it is rather unusual for God's people to be begged to stop giving to an offering. More commonly, a significant proportion of Christians usually need some encouragement to give sufficiently to many important offerings. The coincidence of such amazing generosity and restrained fund-raising as seen in the interaction between Paul's leadership team and the Macedonians is a salutary lesson for leaders and believers in every generation. It challenges believers to give more freely to God-honouring causes. It also warns leaders not to force or wrongfully take advantage of such generosity.

How not to promote giving

Some argue that Christians' reluctance to give willingly and generously to meet ministry needs is what inspires the gimmicky, and sometimes pressured, offering-raising methods adopted in some sections of the Church. Others however attribute these questionable methods to more sinister motives like sheer greed and empire-building on the part of leaders. No matter what the challenges to funding ministries there are, it is vital that the Church rediscovers and embraces bible-centred and God-honouring principles. These are the ones that respect people's freewill while encouraging them to make adequate provision for His kingdom.

It goes against the grain of biblical ethics to force, deceive or blackmail Christians to give to any cause. This is true no matter how worthy the cause may be. It is unfortunate that leaders who use these unethical means sometime quote certain verses of scripture to back up their conduct. They are truthfully not able to say like Paul:

> *3 For the appeal we make does not spring from error or impure motives, nor are we trying to trick you.* *4 On the contrary, we speak as those approved by God to be entrusted with the gospel. We are not trying to please people but God, who tests our hearts. 5 You know* *we never used flattery, nor did we put on a mask to cover up greed — God is our witness.*
>
> 1 Thessalonians 2:3-5

In accordance with the later part of the above scripture, leaders who take advantage of people often flatter them by saying what they know their audience would like to hear about themselves. They also put on a mask of concern for the hearers' well-being and prosperity in order to hide their own greed so as to entice them give inappropriately.

These negative fund-raising practices may be seen by anyone who regularly attends special Christian events or watches Christian television today. We shall be looking at a couple of examples of these manipulations later in our discussion on *Principle 3: Giving should be to the trustworthy and accountable.*

Leaders who manipulate people to give are more likely to be unaccountable in the management of the gifts they receive. These unaccountable practices are also likely to be manifest in other important areas of their lives and ministries. Hence, we must settle it in our hearts that the kind of giving that we want to be a part of is that which is done in a scripturally informed and free manner. This type of giving is what ensures proper provision for God's kingdom, while securing maximum blessings for the givers.

Principle Challenge:
Do you realise how important the motivation of God's love and the enablement of His grace are in faithful and generous giving?

Principle Prayer:
Lord, fill me afresh with grace to love Your people and Your kingdom. Let Your love and grace be my highest inspiration for generous giving now and always. Amen.

Principle 2

Christ is our chief giving example

8 I am not commanding you, but I want to test the sincerity of your love by comparing it with the earnestness of others. 9 For you know the grace of our Lord Jesus Christ, that though he was rich, yet for your sake he became poor, so that you through his poverty might become rich. 10 And here is my judgment about what is best for you in this matter. Last year you were the first not only to give but also to have the desire to do so. 11 Now finish the work, so that your eager willingness to do it may be matched by your completion of it, according to your means. 12 For if the willingness is there, the gift is acceptable according to what one has, not according to what one does not have. 13 Our desire is not that others might be relieved while you are hard pressed, but that there might be equality. 14 At the present time your plenty will supply what they need, so that in turn their plenty will supply what you need. The goal is equality, 15 as it is written: "The one who gathered much did not have too much, and the one who gathered little did not have too little."

2Corinthians 8:8-15 (NIV)

Encouraged giving versus pressured giving

Some may argue that Paul had both the right and the justification, given the serious need of the saints in Jerusalem, to use his God-given apostolic authority to command the Corinthians to give. Rather than pulling his apostolic rank, he chose to base his appeal on the love and sincerity of the Corinthians. Paul understood that there was a delicate balance to be struck between encouraging people to give and pressuring them to do so. This is true even in the face of an important and pressing need. Striking this balance will always be a challenge for any leader who needs to raise resources to do God's work in tough circumstances in all ages. It is therefore beneficial for us to consider the two great examples Paul drew on to properly inspire unforced generosity in the Corinthians:

The first example he cited was the supreme example of Christ himself; He voluntarily divested Himself of the incalculable riches of heaven and came to earth to become poor like us. By becoming immeasurably poorer, He ensured we could receive the richest blessings of heaven. Secondly, he pointed to the self-sacrificing generosity of the Macedonian Church that was demonstrated by their generous giving to the destitute brothers and sisters in Jerusalem in the face of their own poverty.

He then encouraged the Corinthians to finish the good work of collection they had started earlier, but had stopped for some reason he did not explain. He urged them to add diligence to their initial enthusiasm in order to complete the good work they had begun. As he pointed out, desiring and starting a good thing does not necessarily mean the completion of the deed in good time unless diligence is applied until the end. This lesson is relevant in many areas of Christian life where people receive vision and passion to start a good cause, only to abandon it due to reduced internal motivation or external pressures. In order to encourage generosity without compulsion, Paul gave the Corinthians leeway to prepare their offering fairly well in advance of its collection.

Give what you have

Paul urged the Corinthians to give according to their actual means rather than over-stretching themselves to give more than they had. Also, he did not urge them to borrow in order to give even though the cause they were called to support was truly worthy. As he said, if there is first willingness of heart, what one has should be the yardstick for measuring how much should be given. This guideline is shown clearly in Jesus' commentary on the widow who gave two copper coins into the temple offering in Mark 12:41-44:

> *41 Jesus sat down opposite the place where the offerings were put and watched the crowd putting their money into the temple treasury. Many rich people threw in large amounts. 42 But a poor widow came and put in two very small copper coins, worth only a few cents.*

*43 Calling his disciples to him, Jesus said, "**Truly I tell you, this poor widow has put more into the treasury than all the others. 44 They all gave out of their wealth; but she, out of her poverty, put in everything—all she had to live on.**"*

From the above scripture, two relevant lessons can be derived: the first is that just as Jesus sat looking at the offerings being brought to the temple, God is also interested in our giving and is checking to see how faithfully we are doing it. The second lesson is that God measures our giving, not just on the absolute scale of the amount given, as man usually does. He also measures it on the relative scale of how much we had before making the gift.

It should be noted that Jesus did not specifically comment on what motivated the widow to give all she had unlike the rich who only gave a part of what they had. Neither did He say giving all that one has should be the model to follow every time we give. We should also note that even though Jesus appeared to praise the widow for giving all her livelihood, He did not actually condemn the rich for giving only a part of their wealth. He simply noted that she gave all she had to live on while they gave only some of their wealth. The truth is: Jesus would rather have all our hearts and none of our means than have all of our means and only part, or none of our hearts. It is also true that we will give our means to what truly captures our hearts.

How much we have is therefore a very fair indication of how much we can actually afford to give. Another helpful indication is what our circumstances and responsibilities are at the time we are being called to give. The implication of the lessons from the *'Widow's Mite Story'* above is that, as far as the Lord is concerned, the extent of our faithfulness and sacrifice is always much more important than the size of our gifts. Even relatively small gifts, if given in loving sacrifice, can greatly bless and be blessed by the Lord. This truth is further illustrated in the story of the little boy who gave up his lunch to the Lord for the feeding of five thousand people in John 6:1-13.

Give as directed by the Spirit

As previously seen in the widow's story, we are not always called to empty our pockets whenever a worthy offering is being raised. Instead, the widow's example should encourage us to prayerfully discern how we can best honour God in our giving. This will lead to us giving generously as appropriate to our circumstances in light of the needs being presented to us. The key always, is to listen to the Lord ourselves and to ask Him what He wants us to give, or on occasion, not to give.

We must realise that God, in His infinite wisdom, knows our present and future circumstances. He also knows the full extent of the need being presented and what He is, and will be, inspiring others to give to meet their part in it. We can therefore rest confidently in His providential wisdom as He leads us by His Spirit regarding what part we are to play in giving to meet a particular need. For instance, in the example that we are examining, the task of giving to the needy Jerusalem saints did not rest only on individual Corinthian believers, or indeed on the entire Corinthian Church alone. As we know, the Macedonian Churches and the others had been called to do their part in meeting this need. This understanding should liberate us from undue pressure and condemnation in our giving. This is true no matter how great the need presented may be.

Major areas of giving stewardship

Having discussed the above challenges, it would be wise to proceed by considering the major areas where we are called to exercise the stewardship of our material resources in the service of God, His people and kingdom. They are:

1. Your family – It should be obvious to all faithful Christians that we are called to take adequate financial care of our families. Only heaven itself can tell how many Christians drastically fall short in this area of stewardship because they give so much to the church and to other causes; neglecting their families in the process.

Jesus, in rebuking the religious leaders of His day, warned about using irresponsible giving to God as an excuse for neglecting honouring, by taking practical care of, one's parents:

> *9 And he continued, "You have a fine way of setting aside the commands of God in order to observe your own traditions! 10 For Moses said, 'Honor your father and mother,' and, 'Anyone who curses their father or mother is to be put to death.'* **11 But you say that if anyone declares that what might have been used to help their father or mother is Corban (that is, devoted to God) — 12 then you no longer let them do anything for their father or mother.** *13 Thus you nullify the word of God by your tradition that you have handed down. And you do many things like that."*
>
> *Mark 7:9-13*

It is shocking that the religious leaders of Jesus' day were deliberately encouraging people to neglect their family responsibilities in other to ensure that the temple coffers, from which they were profiting, were being filled to overflowing by scripturally disobedient givers. Such inclination and practice should provoke righteous indignation in us too, if and when we see them in today's Church.

Furthermore, Paul emphasised the need to care for our families when he spoke about the responsibility of taking care of one's widows and immediate family in 1 Timothy 5:3-8:

3 Give proper recognition to those widows who are really in need. 4 But if a widow has children or grandchildren, **these should learn first of all to put their religion into practice by caring for their own family and so repaying their parents and grandparents***, for this is pleasing to God…. 8* **Anyone who does not provide for their relatives, and especially for their own household, has denied the faith and is worse than an unbeliever.**

The above scriptures show why we always need to make sure our giving to God and the church do not stop us from fulfilling our duty of care to our families. They show us that it is actually possible to give too much to God and the church, and too little to our families. We can neglect our practical, God-given family responsibilities in our zeal to give and in our ignorance of God's whole counsel about stewardship. We must realise that such neglect actually dishonours God contrary to what our original intention might be!

It should also be noted that provision for our parents and immediate family does not stop at making material provision for their physical needs. Caring for them spiritually and emotionally are also major parts of our responsibly to them. This means making sure we spend regular qualitative time with our spouses, children and parents.

This reminds me of the pain I heard in the voice of a good friend of mine many years ago. He lamented to me that his commitments to work and church had 'prevented' him from visiting his aged parents as regularly as he knew he should. They lived in a small provincial town only a couple of hours from where he was, but he usually went many months without seeing them. He was convicted that it was not enough to send them regular upkeep money when what they wanted above all was for him to come and spend a day or two with them from time to time. The sad fact is that too many zealously committed Christians, like my friend, are guilty of this kind of neglect of their families and need to repent of it.

In most parts of the Church, a lot is being done by the leadership to persuade Christians to give more to 'kingdom' causes. Much more could still be done to encourage God's people to fully live up to the responsibility of taking care of their immediate families.

2. Your local church – All believers should be a part of a local assembly that serves as their home church. This is where they should be receiving their primary spiritual nourishment, discipleship and fellowship on a continuing basis. This is said with the understanding that not all believers will be able to physically get to fellowship meetings on a regular basis due to various challenges like ill-health, displacement and temporarily broken fellowship. Using the internet, radio, TV and other media as means of meeting fellowship needs may be okay on a short-term basis. These media should however not be allowed to become long-term substitutes for face-to-face contact and fellowship with other Christians in a community setting.

Each local church should be alive to its responsibility of helping people struggling with attending fellowship events in any practical way possible. They can do this by ensuring they actively seek reconciliation with members who have pulled away, or have been alienated from fellowship due to some grievances. They can also arrange to give mobility assistance to elderly and infirm people who would otherwise struggle to make it to meetings on their own. The responsibility of getting connected or reconnected with a physical fellowship however still lies with individual believers. They should be determined to be engrafted into a local church and seek all the practical help they need in order to make sure they are in an active fellowship as Hebrews 10:24-25 clearly states:

> *24 And let us consider how we may spur one another on toward love and good deeds, 25 **not giving up meeting together, as some are in the habit of doing**, but encouraging one another—and all the more as you see the Day approaching.*

Every believer in active fellowship has the responsibility of supporting his local church or assembly with his gifts and abilities as stated earlier in 1 Peter 4:10-11. Ephesians 4:16 also states that the body can only grow to its full potential *"as each part does its work"*. People who may be relatively poor and cash-deficient now may still contribute significantly to the church's ministry by serving in other practical ways. It is important that church leaders ensure that poor people are not made to feel like second-class citizens by the way offerings are raised, and by the way people who give significant monies are praised.

An important part of the work each believer is called to do is giving financially in a consistent manner to enable, promote and sustain the ministry of his local church assembly. Many Christians do this by giving tithes (10 percent of income) and offerings to the church on a regular basis. These should be done without pressure, threat and guilt-tripping that are based on slavish attachment to Old Testament laws and other church traditions. Christians are no longer under the law and are therefore not bound to follow the giving commandments that were given to, and were practiced by, Old Testament believers.

Vitally, the New Testament scriptures do not actually prescribe a specific percentage of income or types of gifts like tithes and first-fruit offerings that Christian must give to the church. The giving practices contained in the Old Testament and established church traditions should therefore serve as inspirational guides rather than rigid prescriptions for discerning New Testament believers. Believers should nevertheless be deliberate about setting aside a regular portion of their income to help their local church. Tithing may be a good place to start this – as long as it is done in the spirit of Christian love and liberty. We shall be taking a closer look at the issue of tithing in our discussion of proportional giving in Chapter 4.

The responsibility of supporting the church also extends to doing one's part in funding the church's special projects and outreaches. Anyone who cares to enquire about the actual costs of keeping a church resourced for ministry is likely to be surprised about how much they add up to. We should therefore be diligent to shoulder our own part of the burden of supporting our local church or assembly as committed disciples of Christ; the Master who owns the Church.

3. Other Christian ministries – As discussed when we looked at the example of the Philippians' support of Paul missions earlier, God's people should support ministry beyond that of their local church. These include other churches and para-church organisations that are carrying out specific ministry assignments which may be different in type and reach from those of a local church. They are helping to establish and advance God's kingdom in the wider world in a way a local church is not able to due to limitations of vision, resources and reach.

We should prayerfully consider which of these ministries are worthy of our support by way of occasional or consistent long-term giving. For instance, I know a married couple who consistently support their national Christian radio station and a para-church ministry that aids persecuted Christians all over the world. This kind of consistent monthly support is in addition to their ongoing support of their own church assembly. I also have a friend who spends a substantial part of his income on sponsoring the missionary trips of those called to bring training and equipping to Christian leaders all over the world. Over the years, he has invested a small fortune to facilitate the ministry of a particular organisation that does this. This type of intentional giving is particularly vital for sustaining ministries that do not have a mother-church to regularly fund them.

4. Christian ministers and missionaries – As 1 Corinthians 9:3-14 clearly explains, God has ordained that those who spend their lives preaching the gospel should be financially sustained thereby. Those who bless you by sharing spiritual riches with you are entitled to receive your material blessings in return. As Paul makes it clear in 1Timothy 5:17-18:

> *17 The elders who direct the affairs of the church well **are worthy of double honor, especially those whose work is preaching and teaching.** 18 For Scripture says, "Do not muzzle an ox while it is treading out the grain," and **"The worker deserves his wages."***

It is a shame that some churches and ministries do not care to pay their ministers and staff decent wages in direct disobedience to the above scripture. It should be noted that it is the responsibility of individual believers, as well as the Church as a whole, to ensure that leaders are properly taken care of materially. This will help free them to happily attend to the ministry of the word and prayer without undue distractions. We should specifically target Missionaries who minister outside the context of the local church, often far away from home, for ongoing financial help.

Unfortunately, some churches and Christian ministries have the practice of paying their staff and ministers so poorly that they can barely live above poverty in their local area. A good friend of mine who belonged to a local church that was part of a big denomination made a radical decision a while back; he decided to start paying his tithe directly to his Pastor's account rather than putting it in the offering as usual! He did this because he discovered that his denomination was paying his pastor so poorly that his family, who lived in the expensive city centre close to the church building, was barely able to make ends meet. While this kind of radical action is not recommended for everyone, the example has hopefully shown that the responsibility of taking care of spiritual leaders lies both with the individual believer as well as the church or ministry organisation.

5. The poor and needy – Jesus, in the context of His anointing by Mary at Bethany, said in Mark 14:7:

> *The poor you will always have with you, and you can help them any time you want. But you will not always have me.*

The above verse shows a plain and unpleasant reality: poverty will always be around us. It also shows the responsibility of helping to lift the poor out of poverty by giving to them lies with Christ's followers.

Paul actually said that one of the main reasons why all who are able should work is to give to the needy:

> *Anyone who has been stealing must steal no longer, but must work, doing something useful with their own hands, **that they may have something to share with those in need.***
>
> *Ephesians 4:28*

Sharing with those in need is therefore a major area of financial stewardship to which we have to regularly attend as we will discuss later in a bit more detail. This sharing has at least two major components: The first is to give to relieve the poor's immediate needs. The second is to help them to find a sustainable way out of poverty in the long term. This can be done by either giving directly to the poor, or to individuals, churches and charitable organisations that take care of them. It is encouraging that Jesus himself modelled commitment to relieving the poor in his ministry as scriptures like John 13:29 show. His apostles also continued this practice as can be seen from Acts 20:35 and Galatians 2:9-10.

6. Saving and investment – Setting aside part of one's income for wise saving and investment is another often-neglected area of stewardship by some of God's people. Most, if not all, can save and invest a bit of their income regularly with some planning and discipline.

It should be noted that ethical and biblical investment sometimes conflict with some of the investment opportunities available in the world. Care should therefore be taken to ensure that Christ is being honoured in the investment choices that are made by individual believers. It should also be noted that while saving in a reputable bank is usually secure, there is usually a risk of losing some or all of the capital put into an investment scheme. It is therefore wise to seek counsel from an accredited investment adviser about risk and ethical implications before making investment decisions.

Living sensibly in order to be able to diligently save and invest is somewhat counter-cultural in this present generation. It is one in which a significant number of people habitually live beyond their income due mainly to the coincidence of discontent-fuelled greed and the availability of easy credit. There are various reasons why people become bound in debt, but near the top of that list is yielding to the world's unbridled consumerist culture; continuous acquisition and usage of goods and services far beyond one's income. This means that rather than such people living frugally enough to enable them save or invest some of their income, they keep borrowing to spend and keep recycling their debts.

Christians who get sucked into the debt vortex eventually discover that they are no longer able to live and give as freely as the Lord wants them to. This is because their spending and indebtedness results in them having no income left over to save and invest. These kinds of self-inflicted problems are different from misfortune occasioned by issues like significant ill-health, sudden loss of livelihood and other things that may drag an individual into debt.

Whatever the reasons for getting in debt, it is always helpful to admit that there is a problem as soon as possible. Then, pastoral and professional help should be sought in order to break the cycle of financial bondage and begin recovery. This recovery is often a difficult process that requires diligent commitment for an extended period of time.

It has been noted that putting money in an interest-yielding savings account usually yields the least return for the money saved. Jesus infers this in the parable of the talents; a great parable of the believer's stewardship, in Mathew 25:24-27:

> 24 *"Then the man who had received one bag of gold came. 'Master,' he said, 'I knew that you are a hard man, harvesting where you have not sown and gathering where you have not scattered seed. 25 So I was afraid and went out and hid your gold in the ground. See, here is what belongs to you.'*
> 26 *"His master replied, 'You wicked, lazy servant! So you knew that I harvest where I have not sown and gather where I have not scattered seed? 27 Well then, **you should have put my money on deposit with the bankers, so that when I returned I would have received it back with interest.***

Though the above parable is about the general stewardship of the resources and talents God entrusts us with, it nevertheless may be applied to the investment of our material possessions too. Putting money in a well-run bank as savings is usually the most secure way to keep it, particularly in the short term, but this only yields a minimal return. People who create wealth in the long term are people who dare to invest their 'talents' rather than just bank, or worse still, bury them.

7. Enjoy the blessings – On the surface, it might sound self-indulgent and unspiritual to expend some of our God-given resources to create fun and pleasure for ourselves and others. God actually wants – I dare say expects – us to enjoy all that the He freely gives us. It is therefore right to occasionally use part of the resources He gives us for edifying rest and recreation that is in keeping with our income and station in life. This may involve us enjoying good food, throwing parties, engaging in edifying hobbies, refreshing and enlightening travel.

Even though we should not spend a high percentage of our income on these, we nevertheless need them to enable us live a more balanced, healthy and fulfilling life. Failure to invest regularly in appropriate rest and recreation – which by the way may cost little or nothing – has led many Christians to become weak, irritable and stressed-out. It has even led some to break down emotionally, physically and spiritually! It is no wonder Jesus Himself took time away from the crowd

47

regularly to rest and pray. He also encouraged his disciples to do so as well:

> *Then, because so many people were coming and going that they did not even have a chance to eat, he said to them,* **"Come with me by yourselves to a quiet place and get some rest."**
>
> *Mark 6:31*

In the above example, it does not appear to have cost Jesus and His disciples any significant amount of money to facilitate the rest and refreshing that they needed at that time. They only needed to exercise the discipline of withdrawal to rest instead of simply carrying on in the face of seemingly unending demands of ministry. We may also open ourselves to significant burnout and spiritual attack if we continue running on empty physical, emotional and spiritual tanks without stopping to refill them regularly by meaningful rest and recreation. It is not coincidental that one of the types of tithes instituted by God in the Old Testament was the celebratory tithe as seen in Deuteronomy 14:22-26.

Another danger of not spending appropriately on relaxation and enjoyment is that of developing an *'Older Brother's Syndrome'*. This syndrome leads to us becoming inflexible, legalistic, and intolerant of those who seem to be enjoying the liberty God gives them. This may be seen in the latter part of the 'Parable of the Prodigal Son' in Luke 15:25-32:

48

*25 "Meanwhile, **the older son was in the field**. When he came near the house, he heard music and dancing. 26 So he called one of the servants and asked him what was going on. 27 'Your brother has come,' he replied, 'and **your father has killed the fattened calf** because he has him back safe and sound.'*

*28 "The older brother became angry and refused to go in. So his father went out and pleaded with him. 29 But he answered his father, '**Look! All these years I've been slaving for you and never disobeyed your orders. Yet you never gave me even a young goat so I could celebrate with my friends.** 30 But when this son of yours who has squandered your property with prostitutes comes home, you kill the fattened calf for him!'*

*31 "'My son,' the father said, '**you are always with me, and everything I have is yours.** 32 But we had to celebrate and be glad, because this brother of yours was dead and is alive again; he was lost and is found.'"*

From the above conversation between older son and the father, it is apparent that the older brother had a legalistic and joyless view of his stewardship of his father's resources. He certainly did not have the father's heart of love, forgiveness and joyful celebration. No wonder he found taking a young goat from his father's abundant flock to have a small party with his friends – even with the father's permission – beyond him! It is certainly proper to use some of our God-given resources to facilitate rest, enjoyment and merriment as is regularly appropriate to our individual needs and circumstances.

A note of caution regarding using the resources God had given us for enjoyment: We need to be careful not to live just to please ourselves and thereby neglect our kingdom responsibilities. It is quite possible to move, sometimes imperceptibly over time, to a place where we would rather spend more and more of the resources in our care to 'enjoy' rather than using a significant part of them for other kingdom purposes on a regular basis. The key to balance as always is to keep close to God's Spirit and His word's guidance.

Good stewardship needs planning and budgeting

It is should be fairly obvious from the preceding exploration of the seven main areas of stewardship that honouring all of them adequately often means managing conflicting pulls on our limited resources. You will therefore find in your own experience that properly balancing the unending needs with your limited resources is a tough act. Developing a habit of prayerful and prudent budgeting can substantially help to tackle this challenge. In a budget, we can deliberately allocate resources to the different areas of stewardship from time to time as our incomes and circumstances permit. This budgeting may be done on a monthly, quarterly or other interval appropriate to our income cycle. This helps to ensure that we are at least considering and attending to each area of stewardship as we should.

In practical terms, it is likely that different stewardship areas will receive different levels of attention at different times, depending on the needs arising and the resources available. Some areas of stewardship like family and church responsibilities will require a minimum level of constant attention. Others stewardship areas like enjoying the blessing may only need occasional attention like taking a vacation once or twice a year. There will also be times when one might need to focus more on some areas and less on others depending on the needs, and seasons of life. Thankfully as New Testaments saints, we have the grace of freedom, flexibility and sensitivity to the Spirit to guide us in apportioning our giving.

Boundaries of giving stewardship

Given the above discussions about the areas of stewardship, we will now proceed to look at the limitations or boundaries that may influence what and how much we actually give. In reality, our willingness and ability to give is usually influenced by a variety of dynamically interacting factors. These may be determined by the influences brought to bear on us in the following main areas:

1. Size of wealth and income – Christians who are materially wealthy or have relatively large incomes should be able to give not just sizeably more, but a higher proportion of such wealth to the kingdom. Many researches all over the world however show that the rich usually give proportionally less of their incomes to charity. This reality is probably true for many Christians across the broad spectrum of the Church; if the story of the Widow's Mite is any indication of general reality. This means that it is often the largeness of heart rather than the size of the wallet that determines how generously individuals give.

2. Family responsibilities – Christians who have responsibility of taking care of a family that includes dependent children and elderly ones may need to give proportionally less of their means to outside ministry than those who are single, or have few or no dependants. As we have seen, they have to prioritise beginning charity at home before reaching out to others. Financially independent, retired people who no longer have immediate dependants may also be in a better position to give more than the average to outside causes.

3. Giving grace – Though all Christians are called to give, not all have the same grace of giving. Romans 12:6-8 states:

> 6 *We have different gifts, according to the grace given to each of us. If your gift is prophesying, then prophesy in accordance with your faith; 7 if it is serving, then serve; if it is teaching, then teach; 8 if it is to encourage, then give*

*encouragement; **if it is giving, then give generously**; if it is to lead, do it diligently; if it is to show mercy, do it cheerfully.*

From the above scripture, it is evident that some Christians are uniquely gifted and internally motivated to give proportionally more of their income to deserving causes and people. They therefore find it easier to give more freely than other Christians who are not so gifted, even in similar circumstances. This is not to excuse any who may claim, rightly or wrongly, that they do not have such gifting from giving as they should. Rather, we should recognise God's sovereign wisdom in placing such uniquely gifted individuals among us. Their examples of sacrificial giving should serve to spur us to also do our best.

4. Understanding of stewardship – Christians who have been well-taught about stewardship, and are constantly engaging with God through the scriptures themselves are in a better position to practice faithful and generous giving. They are much less likely to be unwilling to share the blessings they receive. They are also unlikely to fall into the trap of giving their resources away inappropriately, simply because someone tries to manipulate them by threats of curses or entice them with promises of blessings.

5. Passion for particular causes – In general, how passionately stirred we are about the particular cause we are being called to give to helps to determine how generously we give to it. For instance, some Christians are more disposed to contributing towards training and mission events than to building a physical church building – as important as that might be. God may also lay it on our hearts to support particular people and causes at different seasons of our lives. The direction of our consistent generosity is therefore determined in large part by the stirrings of our hearts. These stirrings help to guide our priorities by considerably influencing what and how much to give to particular demands.

6. Love for the Lord – Even in view of the points highlighted above, the greatest determinant of how freely and lovingly we give will be how much in love we are with God and His people. The extent of God's love determined how much He gave us in His son as Jesus Himself states in John 3:16:

> *For God so loved the world that he gave his one and only Son*, *that whoever believes in him shall not perish but have eternal life.*

The extent of our love will therefore also determine how generous we are in our giving, even in the face of personal difficulties. This truth is demonstrated powerfully by selfless example of the Macedonian Churches we are studying.

Give to meet real needs

In the 2 Corinthians 8:13-15 scripture quoted at the head of this chapter, Paul explained that his appeal to the Corinthians was not meant to burden them unduly while relieving others. Rather, he wanted them to share mutually with their Jewish brothers and sisters, who in turn had other riches to share with them – leading to equality. Elsewhere, he teaches that no one should be expected to burden himself with providing for those who have the ability to provide for themselves but refuse to work. As he explains in 2 Thessalonians 3:7-10:

> 7 **For you yourselves know how you ought to follow our example. We were not idle when we were with you, 8 nor did we eat anyone's food without paying for it. On the contrary, we worked night and day, laboring and toiling so that we would not be a burden to any of you.** 9 We did this, not because we do not have the right to such help, but in order to offer ourselves as a model for you to imitate. 10 For even when we were with you, we gave you this rule: **"The one who is unwilling to work shall not eat."**

Giving should therefore be mainly aimed to provide for those genuinely in need as was modelled so graciously by the new Church in Jerusalem in Acts 4:32-35.

> 32 All the believers were one in heart and mind. No one claimed that any of their possessions was their own, but they

shared everything they had. 33 With great power the apostles
continued to testify to the resurrection of the Lord Jesus. ***And***
God's grace was so powerfully at work in them all 34
that there were no needy persons among them. For from
time to time those who owned land or houses sold them,
brought the money from the sales 35 and put it at the
apostles' feet, and it was distributed to anyone who had
need.

Giving should not be used to enable some to become rich or indulgent at the expense of faithful, hard-working givers. This should be true whether or not the people receiving the gifts are prominent leaders or obscure followers in the church. We have a duty to ensure that those we help are not those refusing to take ongoing responsibility for themselves, or are taking undue advantage of the kindness of others. People who are enduringly lazy and wasteful actually disqualify themselves from receiving freely from God's bounty to us!

Another truth that Paul teaches in verses 13 and 14 of 2 Corinthians 8 is the fact that giving and receiving is an interactive and dynamic experience between givers and receivers over time. People who give today may become receivers tomorrow and vice versa. This is particularly true if we do not limit giving and receiving to the exchange of material things as we are often tempted to. For example, those who are materially poor relative to us often have great spiritual and emotional wealth to share with us. Most people who have gone on a missionary trip from 'rich' first world countries to relatively 'poor' third world countries are often staggered at the contentment and unfeigned joy of the indigenes – particularly believers – that they have come to serve. We must therefore be faithful, not just to give to the materially 'needy', but also be open and humble to receive from them so as to broaden our appreciation and enjoyment of God's grace.

Principle Challenge:
How often do you meditate on the extent and implications of the supreme sacrifice of Christ on your stewardship?

Principle Prayer:
Lord, help me to always keep following Your supreme example of sacrificial giving and that of Your loyal followers through the ages, as I obey Your call to meaningfully impact Your kingdom with my life of giving. Amen.

Principle 3

Giving should be to the accountable and trustworthy

16 Thanks be to God, who put into the heart of Titus the same concern I have for you. 17 For Titus not only welcomed our appeal, but he is coming to you with much enthusiasm and on his own initiative. 18 And we are sending along with him the brother who is praised by all the churches for his service to the gospel. 19 What is more, he was chosen by the churches to accompany us as we carry the offering, which we administer in order to honor the Lord himself and to show our eagerness to help. 20 We want to avoid any criticism of the way we administer this liberal gift. 21 For we are taking pains to do what is right, not only in the eyes of the Lord but also in the eyes of man.

22 In addition, we are sending with them our brother who has often proved to us in many ways that he is zealous, and now even more so because of his great confidence in you. 23 As for Titus, he is my partner and co-worker among you; as for our brothers, they are representatives of the churches and an honor to Christ. 24 Therefore show these men the proof of your love and the reason for our pride in you, so that the churches can see it.

2 Corinthians 8:16-24 (NIV)

A model of accountability

Titus was chosen by Paul to travel to collect this welfare offering partly because he was judged to be genuinely interested in the Corinthian Church's welfare. Perhaps more importantly, he was chosen because he had a record of proven diligence in service and integrity of character. The churches were also asked to nominate an unnamed but praiseworthy brother to accompany him. They did this, not just to strengthen accountability, but to also model teamwork in accordance with Jesus' repeated examples in the Gospels. He rarely sent out lone disciples for assignments, even for seemingly mundane tasks like fetching a donkey and preparing a place for supper.

Paul was at pains to ensure that the manner of collection and administration of the offering did not leave room for any hint of dishonesty. He meant this to be clear, not only to God, but also to men. He chose not to say *"I am accountable only to God"* as some ministry leaders indignantly declare when questions are asked about their stewardship. They see most requests for accountability about the use of resources under their care as a personal affront to their integrity even when it is not so. Some of these leaders falsely believe that their gifting and leadership position frees them from the need to give reasonable account to those they lead. In contrast, Paul chose to use his apostolic authority in a clearly open way in order to leave no room for yielding to temptation or the stirring of suspicion. Today's Church desperately needs to

59

learn and follow the openness and accountability that Paul and his team models here. It is particularly needed in those sections of it that are led by gifted but independent leaders.

Christian leaders should lead in accountability

From Paul's example above, it is clear that the primary responsibility for ensuring openness and accountability in the handling of the precious donations God's people make rests with the leaders. They are accountable to both God and to the people who give in His name. The leaders' task is to ensure that ministry needs are clearly communicated to the people being asked to give. They are then to ensure that the resources given are put to the right use and proper accounts are regularly rendered to those who give. Setting up a transparent accounting system and the independent auditing of such accounts on a regular basis definitely help in promoting such faithful stewardship.

It is not biblical for leaders to insist that their followers should just give and let them get on with allocating the donations without having to render any account to them. A friend who was a young leader in an independent denomination told me about a Ministers' Meeting he attended at which the General Overseer of the ministry presided. At the meeting, some of the Pastors communicated the concerns of the church members that the tithes and offerings given to the church were not being used to cater adequately for the welfare needs of members of the church who did the giving. Instead, they were mainly being used by the denomination's headquarters on capital projects and central overheads. The General Overseer got visibly angry at what he perceived to be a slight on his authority and the questioning of his stewardship of church funds. So he indignantly said: *"Tell those of your members who are not satisfied with the way the church finances are being managed to go and pay their tithes and offerings directly to God himself if they do not wish to pay it to the church"*. All the other ministers present then kept quiet because they felt intimidated by the General Overseer. Even though the issue was not resolved, no one wanted to risk being labelled a rebel!

The above experience contrasts sharply with that of another friend who had recently moved to a new town as a result of getting married and joining her husband in his church. Asked how she was finding her new church, she told how surprised she was that the practices of her new church radically differed from those of previous ones. These differences led her to re-examine her doctrine of church and the expectations of the way things are done within it. She said: *"I have found that a lot of the things I took for granted as biblical church culture were actually man-made practices inspired by our own culture"*. She cited, as an example, the shock she experience when she attended an annual Church Business Meeting in which the church's audited accounts were shared and discussed openly with the members. It was the very first time that had happened in her decade-plus experience of church!

Yet another friend recently expressed his surprise at the fact that the Lead Pastor of his new church announced, to the last penny, exactly how much was raised during a special offering. He was also surprised that the Pastor regularly tells the church how such collected monies were being spent.

Givers should seek accountability

The above examples illustrate why it is also important for Christian givers to help keep leaders accountable in their handling of the gifts they receive. Sometimes God's people fail to ask questions, even in a spirit of love and humility, because they are afraid of offending the 'Lord's Anointed'. He is all-too-often a sole, charismatic leader who is expected to hear from God and give instructions to the church. He is usually regarded as infallible and unquestionable, so anyone who attempts to question any of his actions and decisions is likely to be regarded as opposing God's specially chosen one.

Some Christians also hold back from asking the right questions about accountability because they do not wish to be regarded as trouble-makers, or people seen to be questioning the integrity of their leaders. Some however do not really care how donated funds are used; provided they perceive that they are being, or will be blessed and prospered, as a result of their giving.

Other believers give questionable offerings because they are swayed by the charisma of the apparently gifted preacher asking for such offerings. This is in addition to the fact that such believers are often promised immediate miracles and breakthroughs if only they would 'sow a seed' offering in order to receive an 'anointed blessing' being supposedly released by the charismatic preacher. Yielding to such enticement of self-interest has led countless believers to part with their worldly goods in the hope of exchanging them for multiplied returns of goods and miracles. They do this despite the fact that God has already made provision to freely bless His people richly for their enjoyment and for the benefit of His kingdom.

Sowing Seeds of Error

A dangerous and continuing error that some of our current Christian generation have bought into wholesale is this: God requires us to first pay him some sort of special offering or sow a seed before He can intervene in our affairs to meet a need or bestow a special blessing on us. This is a grotesque distortion of the biblical sowing and reaping truth as it relates to giving and receiving. This distortion stretches the truth beyond the bounds of scripture by turning God into a sort of cosmic slot machine who guarantees to pay big when people put some money into it. This kind of understanding is promoted by ministers seeking to exploit the gullibility of ignorant, needy and sometimes greedy people of God.

It is enlightening that in James' discussion of the reasons for unfulfilled longings in the life of God's people, he did not attribute such lack to the fact that they did not sow seeds to secure God's blessings. Rather, he said:

> *2 You desire but do not have, so you kill. You covet but you cannot get what you want, so you quarrel and fight.* **You do not have because you do not ask God. 3 When you ask, you do not receive, because you ask with wrong motives,** *that you may spend what you get on your pleasures.*
>
> James 4:2-3

It is clear from the above that not asking explicitly in faith and asking for the wrong motives are the major reasons for lack of divine provision in the lives of God's people. Other reasons mentioned in the Bible include lack of faith, not repenting from specific sin and not forgiving others.

It is true that God sometimes calls us to give materially to Him in order to release us from the hold of what we have, and to make room for greater blessings from Him. The fact is that some of those blessings will be bestowed on us anyway, whether or not we give to a particular offering. One of the reasons God may sometime inspire us to give in a particularly generous way in certain instances is because He knows that a big blessing, which will put our giving in the shade is on the way! However, it is not true that we can simply desire anything, give an offering or seed for it, and have God to do it for us irrespective of His sovereign purpose and our heart's condition. It is also not true that we have to pay God materially in advance before He blesses us materially or by other means. The scriptures are clear that all of the blessings of God are made available to us based on the grace and mercy of Christ. It is in Him that all of God's multi-dimensional promises of blessings find their positive confirmation (2 Corinthians 1:20).

It is a sad reality that some preachers have built apparently wealthy ministries by peddling promises of immediate and abundant reaping for material seeds sown. This kind of distortion of the gospel message for personal gain and kingdom-building is by no means a new phenomenon as some of today's people may think; such was in existence even in Paul's days as he states in 2 Corinthians 2:17:

> **Unlike so many, we do not peddle the word of God for profit.** *On the contrary, in Christ we speak before God with sincerity, as those sent from God.*

He further affirms in 2 Corinthians 4: 2:

> *Rather, we have renounced secret and shameful ways;* **we do not use deception, nor do we distort the word of God.** *On the contrary, by setting forth the truth plainly we commend ourselves to everyone's conscience in the sight of God.*

The methods by which such preachers *"distort the word of God"* in order to make people give are so numerous and inventive that doing them justice will need a book of its own!

We will therefore look at just one example that someone shared recently:

He attended a special meeting in which a prominent charismatic preacher was invited to preach. The preacher proceeded to preach on generational iniquities and the curses resulting from them. He made it clear that the consequences of these iniquities, which passed down the bloodline, were very real in the lives of his Christian audience today. He then affirmed that the curses were preventing them from enjoying the full prosperity that was theirs in God. The solution he came up with was for the believers in the meeting to bring three separate sacrificial offerings; one for each of the past three generations. This was in order for them to have the curses of each generation broken off them by him. He further said that they should bring monetary offerings bigger than those used to establish the original sacrifices and covenants still troubling them. This was in spite of the fact that there was no way his listeners could determine or even fairly estimate the worth of the sacrifices supposedly made against them generations before they were even born.

He did not teach these believers their position and inheritance as New Creatures based on the superior new covenant established by the sacrificial shedding of the blood of Jesus and His subsequent resurrection. Instead, his solution for victory was based exclusively on paying money for the freedom they had been convinced they needed, rather than appropriating the finished work of Christ for it! Many of the people in his audience subsequently flocked out to give the requested offerings in return for spiritual freedom and material prosperity. They, sadly, were obviously undiscerning of the unsound theology and suspect motive on which his preaching was based.

The saddest thing about this kind of error is not that it robs God's people of their material resources, but that it completely misleads them to put their faith in damaging falsehood. It is no wonder that Christians who receive such false teaching think, talk and live like the unredeemed! They develop distorted mind-sets that get them caught in the unenviable web of trying to earn by works what God has freely made available to them by Christ's grace. This is a disguised form of legalism and commercialisation of the gospel that robs the gospel of God's power and diverts God's people into blind alleys of unprofitable commerce. They unfortunately fail to grasp the truth that a friend recently expressed: *"God gives to us freely based on the grace that is ours in Christ; He is not in the business of selling His protection and blessings"*. This assertion agrees with Jesus' instruction to His apostles as He sent them out on mission in the account in Matthew 10:8 "

...freely you have received, freely give".

It is always right to support Christian organisations and churches that do beneficial ministry with our resources. It is however wrong to be made to pay for the ministry like you would for a business transaction. Jesus vehemently condemned the religious leaders of His day for commercialising worship and diminishing genuine consecration to God thereby. He, the gentle Son of God was indignant enough to take up a whip to cleanse the temple because of this!

God holds you accountable for your giving

It is a fact that God's people face regular pressure to give to all kinds of people, causes and organisations. It is nevertheless pertinent for them to realise that He holds them accountable for what they give and how they give it. God is not pleased when we carelessly give His resources in our care to those who are likely to misuse, misappropriate, or sometimes outrightly embezzle them. It is therefore our spiritual responsibility to constantly exercise discernment in our giving. This is to ensure that as much as it is in our power, what we give is actually helping to advance God's kingdom rather someone's private one.

If we are honest, we will probably admit that we have given without proper discernment or with improper motives in the past. Today, God freely offers us forgiveness for those past mistakes, but He expects us to rely on His wisdom and grace to stop making such mistakes in the future. He wants His resources in our care channelled into the best places and put into the best hands for the building up of His kingdom.

It should be noted that holding Christian leadership accountable does not mean we should become accusatory, disrespectful or nit-pick at the finances of the ministries and churches we support. Rather, we should aim to ensure that there are appropriate accountability processes in place, and that the church or ministry's orientation and direction of travel is towards integrity and accountability. For instance, a church or ministry that subscribes to an independent financial oversight organisation like the Evangelical Council for Financial Accountability (ECFA) is more likely to be run uprightly. This is an extra level of financial oversight that gives discerning donors confidence that their donations will be used appropriately.

Accountability benefits all

It is vital to acknowledge that establishing transparency and accountability in the handling of finances does not just benefit the givers and God's Kingdom in general. It is also particularly beneficial to the leaders who manage those resources as well! This is because they are less likely to fall into the temptation of misappropriating or stealing funds in their trust as there is a pre-established system by which they have to regularly account for their use.

A situation where the church or ministry's finances are not clearly demarcated from the leaders' personal finances is likely to result in abuse sooner or later. Churches and ministries staff are also less likely to succumb to the temptation to waste, misappropriate or steal ministry funds if they know that there is a robust accounting and auditing system in place.

Another benefit of good financial accountability is its usefulness in helping the ministry to plan, review and execute the deployment of resources more efficiently and prudently. These important stewardship obligations are easier to fulfil where there are adequate records and processes on which to properly base them. Such accountability helps to build up the ministry's credibility in the esteem of its supporters, partners and the outside world.

Discerning and wise Christians should be reluctant to support ministries and churches where transparent accountability is not the norm. It should be settled in our hearts that God is not glorified, and His kingdom and people are not benefited truly and fully, when we give to unaccountable people and organisations.

Principle Challenge:
How regularly do you evaluate how much of your giving actually goes to Christ-honouring causes and people?

Principle Prayer:
Lord, please help me to avoid the pitfalls of giving the material resources You have entrusted me with to people and organisations that are likely to steal or misuse them. Amen.

Principle 4

Prepared giving is best

1. There is no need for me to write to you about this service to the Lord's people. 2 For I know your eagerness to help, and I have been boasting about it to the Macedonians, telling them that since last year you in Achaia were ready to give; and your enthusiasm has stirred most of them to action. 3 But I am sending the brothers in order that our boasting about you in this matter should not prove hollow, but that you may be ready, as I said you would be. 4 For if any Macedonians come with me and find you unprepared, we—not to say anything about you—would be ashamed of having been so confident. 5 So I thought it necessary to urge the brothers to visit you in advance and finish the arrangements for the generous gift you had promised. Then it will be ready as a generous gift, not as one grudgingly given.

2 Corinthians 9:1-5, NIV

Finish what was started

The Corinthian saints had inspired others, the Macedonians included, by their initial eagerness to give to this welfare fund but had failed to follow through on their commitment. Theirs is a sad example of Christians who enthusiastically discern the will of God in a particular area of life and passionately commit to fulfilling it, only to fade away from such commitment when the distractions and challenges of life barge in on them. We are not told why the Corinthians did not finalise their initial commitment, but the net result was that the aid they promised was not ready for delivery when it should have been.

Paul was therefore encouraging them by this letter, and by sending Titus and friends, to follow through on their earlier commitment to give. He urged them to prepare their gift in advance of its collection in order to make it easier for them to give willingly from the heart rather than from a sense of forced obligation. He had instructed them to do this in a former letter when he said in 1 Corinthians 16:2:

> *On the first day of every week,* **each one of you should set aside a sum of money in keeping with your income,** *saving it up, so that when I come no collections will have to be made.*

Unforced giving

It is notable that in making the appeal for this offering, Paul neither imposed a levy nor suggested a specific amount for all the Corinthians to give. Rather, he left it to individuals saints to determine what to set aside weekly for the offering, depending on how God blessed them each week. This meant that the relatively poorer saints did not feel pressured to give a certain minimum, which some of them might have struggled to afford. Conversely, the richer ones did not have room to feel smugly satisfied about having *'done their bit'* by giving up to or even somewhat above the minimum levy, when they may well have done more.

Leaving how much to contribute to each person's conscience and judgment is arguably a risky way to raise money. This is because there is always the possibility that what people give voluntarily may fall short of the target expected. It is nevertheless the surest way to see the practical demonstration of unforced giving grace among love-motivated New Testament believers. It is always helpful, in this respect, for the leadership to clearly communicate the type and extent of the need to the people being asked to give beforehand. Paul had done this in his previous communication with the Corinthians about the plight of the Church in Jerusalem.

The explanation above does not mean that levying a minimum amount for all to give to an offering is always wrong. This approach may be appropriate in cases where there is a specific amount to be raised and the people being called to give equally have similar economic capabilities. It may also be appropriate where the amount levied is small enough to be easily affordable by all being asked to pay it. Having said this, it may yet be argued that people with similar economic capabilities are unlikely to have similar life circumstances and motivations affecting how much they can give at any particular time. These are important reasons why levying specific amounts should be done rarely and cautiously as it has the potential to hinder rather than promote God's grace in this vital area of stewardship. When it comes to giving, equal sacrifice rather than equal amounts should always be the aim.

Give proportional to your means

Paul further introduces the vital concept of proportionality as a guide to how much Christians should give to meet presenting needs. He linked how much to be contributed by individuals directly to how much each receives as income per period – weekly in this particular case – from the Lord. It assumes crucially that what you are able to make through your legitimate work and investments is actually a blessing from the Lord; rather than just being results of your own wisdom and hard work!

Proportional giving had been established even before New Testament times as was reflected in the detailed ordinances of the giving of the tithe (10% of income) and other offerings established for Old Testament believers. It should be noted that even though all of them were commanded to tithe, they were given leeway to give some offerings based on their personal willingness and economic power. For instance Jesus' relatively poor parents, who by the way, were at the time still Old Testament believers – if we understand that the New Testament actually inaugurated by the death and resurrection of Jesus – offered two turtle doves instead of a lamb and a dove at his dedication in the temple.

They did this in accordance with the requirements laid out in Leviticus 12: 2 – 6.

Even though Christians are no longer bound by the law to give tithes and offerings like the Jews of old, adopting some of their giving patterns as a form of regular proportional giving to God may still be helpful to today's Christians in expressing their stewardship. This is true, provided those giving according to such patterns understand the freedom they have in Christ's grace. Failure to acknowledge Christ's love and liberty in this area will ultimately lead into believers falling into the trap of unprofitable and inflexible observance of the law from which Christ has freed them. Paul makes this point clearly in scriptures like Galatians 3:1-10 and Romans 7:1-6. We will now go on to briefly explore what the Bible has to say about tithing in particular.

Tithing in the Old Testament

Abraham was the first person who is recorded to have paid the tithe in the Old Testament in Genesis 14: 17-20. He voluntarily offered the tithe to Melchizedek, the King of Salem, after he met him on the way back from a victorious military campaign. He had managed to rescue his cousin Lot and got many spoils of war in addition. Two things are noteworthy about this encounter: the first is that the tithe paid by Abraham was done voluntarily without a commandment to do so. The second is that it was paid from the spoils of war and not from Abraham's personal wealth.

Later in Genesis 28: 16-22, Jacob vowed to pay the tithe of all that he would be given; if God kept him, provided for him on his journey and ensured his safe return. Again, there are two things worthy of note in this particular case: the first is that it was Jacob who voluntarily vowed to tithe rather than being commanded to do so. The second, and perhaps more significant point, is the fact that vowing the tithe in exchange for divine blessing and protection was not really necessary. This is because God had just appeared to him in a dream and promised to do the very same thing Jacob was vowing for in Gen 28: 12-15! Somehow, Jacob failed to realize that God – because of His faithfulness to the Abrahamic Covenant – was committed to aiding and blessing him despite the fact that he was not a particularly upright man. Though we do not know for sure whether Jacob fulfilled his tithe vow, it is reasonable to assume he did.

These two examples of tithing before the law showed that the Patriarchs paid the tithe on their own volition in gratitude for blessings already received, as it was in the case of Abraham, or for blessings requested, as it was in Jacob's case.

It was not until the law was instituted through Moses that paying the tithe became a commandment for all God's covenant people as Numbers 18:20-28 and Leviticus 27:30-33 show. The tithe was to be paid from agricultural products;

the harvest of crops and the increase of animals. It was not a tithe of money as it has evolved to be today.

God's purpose for instituting the tithe as part of the law can be discerned from the types of tithes He asked His people to bring. The three types of tithes instituted by God are:

1. **Levitical or Sacred Tithe**: To provide for Levites and Priests who had no land allocated to them like other Israelites. They were expected to fully dedicate their lives to serving God and the people without the distractions of trying to make a living without such support (Numbers 18:20-24).

2. **Celebration Tithe**: For feasting in the Lord's presence with family, friends and the poor. By this, God was effectively asking His people to use their tithe to occasionally throw a party before Him! (Deuteronomy 14:22-26).

3. **Welfare Tithe**: To provide for the welfare of strangers, orphans and widows who would otherwise be impoverished. This was to be distributed to the poor at the end of every third year (Deuteronomy 14:28-29).

Tithing in the New Testament

There are three major references to tithing in the New Testament. Interestingly, these references actually refer to what was done in Old Testament times. You will find this particularly agreeable if you understand that the New

Testament did not actually start until the Church was birthed after Jesus' death and resurrection. The time in which Jesus lived was actually a transition time between the Old and New Testaments in which the old practices and traditions dominated. Even John the Baptist was described by Jesus in Luke 7:27-29 as the greatest Old Testament Prophet. He was nevertheless said to be positionally inferior to the least New Testament saint, in Christ's coming kingdom!

The first reference was when Jesus rebuked the Pharisees for practicing an extreme form of tithing while neglecting the weightier matters of the law in Matthew 23:23-24 and Luke 11:42. They had degenerated to tithing even small amounts of spices in their quest for meticulous compliance with the law. They had however neglected to practice justice, mercy and faithfulness which were God's original objectives for instituting the law.

The second reference was in a parable rebuking the pious but falsely self-righteous Pharisees in Luke 18: 11-13. Again, this was based on their meticulous adherence to legalistic tithing without love and humility. In these two instances, Jesus' aim as revealed in His words, was to rebuke the Jewish leaders' extreme and legalistic adherence to the letter of the law while violating its spirit – which was God's original intention and purpose for it.

The third, and only time in the Epistles, was when the writer of Hebrews argued for the supremacy of the priesthood of Christ – after the order of Melchizedek – over that of Aaron and the Levites in Hebrews 7. His major point was that the Levitical priesthood has now been set aside and replaced with the supreme and unending priesthood of Christ.

A careful reading of these text shows that it affirms the fact that Abraham – and Levi by extension – voluntarily gave a tithe to Melchizedek who was able to bless him. The writer's focus was showing the superiority of Melchizedek the tithe-receiving Priest, who was a type of the eternal Christ, to the now terminated Levitical priesthood. It does not suggest that, or command New Testament saints to pay the tithe. This is probably the only verse in the New Testament scripture from which voluntary giving of tithes may be inferred. It was however not the point that the writer of Hebrews made in his discussions.

Even though the Acts of the Apostles and the Epistles are silent on tithing except for the lone Hebrew reference above, they have so much to say about giving in general, as we have begun to see. We have been exploring the various ways in which the early Church used their material means to support God's kingdom and His people, and will continue to do so, throughout this study.

A good question to ask, in light of the above discussions, is this: *"Why did tithing become a traditional practice in parts of the Church even though it was not commanded by Christ and His Apostles.?"* There is no clear or certain answer to this question but it is likely that the practice of tithing was carried over from the Jewish religion by the first Jewish converts. Scriptures like Acts 21:17-26 show clearly that some of the original Jewish believers were zealous about keeping the laws of Moses. This made them hang on to a lot of the old Jewish practices that they had grown up with. Their insistence that Gentile converts conform to these old practices, like circumcision, caused a lot of friction in the early Church. It even threatened its unity and growth but for the wise and timely intervention of the Apostles and Elders who led the Church as Acts 15 clearly shows. On a positive note, they probably found this particular tradition useful in funding the Church as many will no doubt testify even today.

In summary, the tithe was supposed to be used to support the Levite ministers, to aid the poor and for feasting in celebration before the Lord. Consequently, the prioritisation and practical expression of our giving should be made to reflect these areas in order for us to please our Master.

In today's church the payment of tithe is often taught, stressed and sometimes enforced as a commandment even though there is no such commandment, whether explicit or implicit, in the New Testament as it was in the Old. This does not mean believers may not be encouraged to tithe with the same volunteer spirit like the Old Testament Patriarchs. If rightly administered, the tithe is still useful to support Christian workers and their work. Tithing can also help believers to establish a habit of faithful and consistent stewardship of the resources God blesses them with as many who do so will testify. Such tithing should however be done without compulsion or threats of curses like it is the case in some churches today.

Allow people time to prepare their gifts

It is good practice for Christians to be given both time and mental space to prepare their offerings ahead of its collection. The obvious exception is when there is an urgent need for which an immediate response is necessary. It is vital for ministry leaders to realise that while pressured and immediate giving may bring resources in quickly and bountifully, it often does not benefit the kingdom in the long term. This is because it robs the givers of the ability to consider their giving critically and properly express their generosity in a way that honours Christ and helps them develops a lifestyle of free generosity. This kind of considered giving is what sustains faithful and joyful generosity among believers in the long term.

As a young believer, I attended a yearly convention meeting of a church at which a prominent preacher was the guest speaker. After preaching late into that night, he proceeded to raise a special offering. A lot of people were already preparing to leave because it was late and the venue was a little way out of town for most attendees. When he saw that people were beginning to leave, he ordered them not to leave without giving into the offering that night, saying: *"You must not leave until this offering has been collected because your future financial destiny is at risk if you do not give sacrificially into it"*. Even though I, like some others, had my offering prepared and was ready to leave it with the ushers on the way out, I felt really uncomfortable with the perceived threat in his voice. He seemed to be implying that God's people had no positive financial future unless they gave bountifully to the offering that particular night. This was irrespective of whatever else may be going on in their hearts and lives. Looking back, I feel generosity could have simply been encouraged without the perceivable threat that accompanied his offering appeal. The preacher probably had good intentions, but the way he made the appeal ended up portraying God as a vengeful 'Mafia Don' who was out to 'get' those who did not pay him his protection money immediately and fully.

Prepare to give

Thankfully, most of the giving we do in church is non-urgent, so there is usually ample room for believers to prepare to give faithfully as part of regular worship. We should not, for example, rumble around for some loose change to drop in the offering bag or plate during regular worship services. Instead, it is wise and helpful to make a personal decision to budget specifically for your weekly offerings in church. Hopefully you will sometimes give beyond what you budget during worship, and rarely below that amount. This amount will also hopefully change progressively with your circumstances over the years. It is also useful to follow this guidance when preparing to attend a special meeting or occasion where an offering is likely to be taken.

Believers who take God and His kingdom seriously are more likely to make it a duty to prepare to give generously as part of their worship. It is one of the surest ways to demonstrate love and loyalty to the Master who bought them to be His very own. They also view this type of consistent giving as a means of storing their treasures in heaven whilst advancing the kingdom on earth.

David exemplified this good practice in his preparations for the temple building. He expressed it in his parting charge to Solomon before his death in 1 Chronicles 22:14-16:

> *"**I have taken great pains to provide for the temple of the LORD** a hundred thousand talents of gold, a million talents of silver, quantities of bronze and iron too great to be weighed, and wood and stone. And you may add to them. 15 You have many workers: stonecutters, masons and carpenters, as well as those skilled in every kind of work 16 in gold and silver, bronze and iron—craftsmen beyond number. Now begin the work, and the LORD be with you."*

We should do our best to consistently follow David's example by being careful to make provision for the house and people of God in our giving. Not being careful to prepare our giving may result in our becoming unfaithful stewards of God's abounding grace to us.

Another great advantage of prayerfully preparing what to give in advance is that you are much less likely to succumb to pressure and manipulation to give what is not appropriate. A helpful addition to this is that even after you have pre-determined what to give in a meeting or to a cause; you should still be open to listen for divine guidance to give differently. God should always be allowed His right to lead you to do more or less than you prepared to do!

Principle Challenge:
How deliberate and intentional are you about preparing your regular giving?

Principle Prayer:
Lord, help me to be diligent in setting aside some of my means to provide for Your people and Kingdom in a consistent and systematic way. Amen.

Principle 5

Hilarious giving is best

6 Remember this: Whoever sows sparingly will also reap sparingly, and whoever sows generously will also reap generously. 7 Each of you should give what you have decided in your heart to give, not reluctantly or under compulsion, for God loves a cheerful giver.

2 Corinthians 9:6-7, NIV

Giving is sowing

Paul reminded the Corinthians, as he had probably taught them previously, that giving is a form of sowing which yields a harvest that is proportional to the amount of seed sown. A farmer who wants a big harvest would be best advised to plant as much good quality seed as he can. One who is content with a small harvest need not however bother too much about the quantity and quality of his seed. Good quality soil is also a necessity for a good harvest so that the seed planted can have a good base to grow and flourish. Accordingly, Christian giving can be seen at least in part, as an investment that can yield profitable future returns. These returns may include, but is not limited to, material blessings as will be examined in detail in the next chapter on *'Giving's reward'*.

It should be noted that just as all physical seeds sown do not have the same harvest period, not all our material seeds will bring an immediate harvest. There are seeds we sow today that will not be ready for harvest until much later in the future; some for many months and years to come. We should therefore continue to give freely and faithfully even when we seem not to get an immediate harvest. Our faithful and persistent giving actually helps to water and tend our seeds for harvest as Paul encourages in Galatians 6:9. The need of patience for harvest is one more reason not to be deceived by those who ask people to give in order to guarantee an immediate one.

Give hilariously

The vital insights into the rewards of sowing shared above were aimed at encouraging the Corinthians to give generously. In addition, Paul was quick to point out that a happy – literally hilarious – disposition of heart was equally vital to acceptable giving in God's sight. He recognises that it is every bit possible to give, not out of the overflow of a generous heart, but from one of grudging resentment. The really good news is that God bestows Spirit-inspired joy upon His children irrespective of their circumstances. He further looks for that joy to be reflected in their giving.

We can, and should, keep giving joyfully like the Macedonians, even when the circumstances surrounding us are less than happy as measured on a human happiness index. This joy will be promoted by the persuasion that what we are giving is proper and will truly benefit God's kingdom and people.

Why we give wrongfully?

The reasons why believers fail to give correctly and joyfully are as varied as they are mixed. Some see giving as a religious obligation they simply have to fulfil. Others give because they feel a compulsion to do so by pressure exerted by leaders that they look up to. Some also give joylessly because they have been cleverly manipulated or threatened to do so. Others give grudgingly because they have not been given time to prepare for a non-urgent offering. The last main reason is selfish greed; focusing mainly on the prosperity and miraculous breakthrough that will be theirs as a reward for their giving. They do this even though a spiritually discerning person should be able to see that the way the offering is being raised is not Christ-honouring. All these reasons have the ability to stifle or corrupt the faithful benevolence of God's people and so make their gifts less acceptable to God.

Does God ever bless those who give from wrong motives?

A good question to ask is this, given the wrong motives for giving enumerated above: *"Does God ever bless people who give with wrong motives or in wrong ways?"* I believe that the answer to this question is 'Yes, but probably No'. It may be 'Yes' because God is a gracious and merciful God who understands the human frailties that sometimes prevent us from giving rightly and from the best motives. The fact is that He longs to bless us, whether we give materially or not, so He sometimes does so even if our motivations and actions are somewhat dubious. He however wants us to grow up in our understanding of His purposes as it relates to our stewardship. He also continually strives to purify our motives by the in-working of His Spirit. As Paul warns in Romans 2:4-6, God's kindness should lead us to repentance instead of affirming us in our self-seeking errors.

His answer may therefore be 'No' if we wilfully persist in ignorance, disobedience and error. He may choose not to bless us as we expect no matter how much we give. For instance, believers who persist in just 'giving to receive', instead of living a wholesome life of loving obedience may be setting themselves up for an unpleasant experience from His hand of discipline. While it is true that God uses our giving as a means of bringing His blessings into our lives, we cannot deceive or bribe Him into blessing us. This is true no matter what, and how much we give to get into His good books. Hence, we must constantly evaluate our giving in the light of His word and Spirit in order to ensure that we measure up to His revealed will and purpose. We must never forget that though God longs to pour His blessings into our lives, He still reserves the sovereign right to determine the type, extent and timing of such blessings.

Giving can be painful yet joyful

The principle of hilarious giving raises another key question: *"Can an offering be acceptable to God if you are 'unhappy' because of feeling the 'pain in the offering' as you give it?"* In answering this, it is vital to first realise that God can differentiate between the genuine pains of sacrifice and that of a heart wilfully rebelling against His will for us and His kingdom.

On a personal note, one of the toughest giving decisions I ever had to make was to give away the first Bible that I bought after committing to Christ in my late teens. I had read and marked virtually every page of it in coloured crayon within a couple of years. I was so familiar with its layout and my colour-coded markings that I could open most portions of scripture in double-quick time.

In my third year in the university I was privileged to share a room with a freshman who was a young and vibrant believer. I lent him that Bible for some time and he fell in love with it. When the loan period was over, he asked me if he could keep it. I initially refused and even offered to buy him another one, but he persisted, saying he preferred that particular one. In the end, I let him have it even though it broke my heart to give away my irreplaceable 'first-love' Bible. I was pained at losing a treasured possession that was a significant token of my early walk with God. I was nevertheless glad a precious brother, whose fellowship I still cherish today was going to have it. This fact gave me joy even though I was sad to give it up.

The experience above hopefully shows that as contradictory as it might initially sound, there are times when sorrow and joy mix together in our giving. This is particularly so when we choose to give up something needed or treasured because of a sense of commitment to a higher purpose.

Sowing in tears

Even though most of the sowing we do does not involve tears, some sowing does involve tears as Psalm 126:6 says:

Those who go out weeping,
carrying seed to sow,
will return with songs of joy,
carrying sheaves with them.

Sowing such precious seed, instead of keeping or eating it can be a daunting experience. This is true even for a mature believer – particularly in lean times. Those who release such seed may however experience God's miraculous and abundant provisions in unusual ways like the Widow of Zarepath did in 1 Kings 17:7-16. As we have discussed, God sees beyond our pain to the actual inspiration of the pain, be it a sense of loss, or just plain selfish disobedience. Based on His discernment of the often mixed motivations behind our giving, He rewards our faithfulness in obeying His promptings. He is faithful to do this even when we do so against our selfish natural inclinations.

The Lord empathises with the unavoidable pain and human anxiety we often experience in the process of sacrificial giving. The encouraging thing is that the more we yield to God and enjoy His goodness, the more joyfully we can give. We then progressively find out that we can more easily scale heights of sacrifice that were previously difficult for us as we increasingly enjoy more of His liberty. We also mature emotionally and spiritually as we learn to joyfully part with material things for the sake of the kingdom. This results in our becoming freer and more truly blessed citizens of the Kingdom.

Principle Challenge:
How well are you learning to be a joy-filled giver even when you have to sacrifice to do so?

Principle Prayer:
Lord, please help me to become a more joyful and enthusiastic giver to Your people and Kingdom, even when giving is painful. Amen.

Principle 6

God always outgives the giver

And God is able to bless you abundantly, so that in all
things at all times, having all that you need, you will
abound in every good work.

2 Corinthians 9:8 (NIV)

Abounding blessing

What Paul describes in the above scripture is a wonderful
level of abundance in which God lifts you way above just
having enough to keep your head above the water. It means
being brought to the place where you are able to freely dish
out His generous provisions on a regular basis. This is
because you have been blessed with more than enough, and
have grown liberal in distributing the abundance of grace
that you receive!

The level of provision described here is so fantastic that
most Christians think it a fantasy when compared with the
reality of their present lives. Paul was however inspired to
write this because it is not only a real possibility, but it is
what God wants for, and can do for, us!

This does not mean every faithful giver will become
materially wealthy overnight. Some may however eventually
become materially rich as they faithfully and consistently
invest their 'talents' by using the sound biblical principles of

diligent stewardship. Paul was in effect saying that God, in His gracious generosity wishes to lift His faithful children, who are committed to the cause of His kingdom, to a place where they can contribute significantly to every real kingdom need He wishes them to meet.

More than we can ask or think

The above insights into divinely bestowed abundance should remind us of the mind-blowing possibilities declared in Paul's exclamation of revelation and praise in Ephesians 3:20-21:

> *20 Now to him **who is able to do immeasurably more than all we ask or imagine, according to his power that is at work within us**, 21 to him be glory in the church and in Christ Jesus throughout all generations, for ever and ever! Amen.*

God is both creative and comprehensive in the way He rewards our giving, so we may rest secure in His wise providence. He gives, not just quantitatively in material terms, but qualitatively in many non-material ways.

This truth about the God who gives so exceedingly always reminds me of one of my maternal grandmother's favourite praise-names for God; she used to hail him as "the God who knows how to answer better than one can ask". This sometimes means God's reward or blessing for our material giving is not just simply giving back multiplied material blessings in return. He might, for example, choose to bless the giver with peace and a wise insight into a particularly difficult situation instead of with money. It should also be acknowledged that God reserves the right not to give anything back for any particular gift we supposedly 'give' to Him. These are some of the main reasons why the simplistic expectation of 'multiple' or 'hundredfold return' for every material gift given, as is preached in some sections of the church, does not usually work for those who give with such an expectation.

People who preach that God's people should always expect geometric, like-for-like material reward for their gifts usually do so by cherry-picking a few favourable scriptures. They then spice the scriptures up with some testimonies of people who are said to have experienced immediate 'wonderful miraculous provision' by their giving. What these preachers usually fail to say is that the testimonies – even when they are true – are often the exceptions rather than the rule. We must therefore humbly and wisely realise that God is not an Automatic Teller Machine (ATM) into which we can slot a card, press a few pre-set buttons and expect a particular amount to come out based on the 'seed' we have put in the account.

How to meet needs

Maturing Christians need to realise that they are not always called to personally meet every need they know of. The fact that you know of a need does not automatically mean you are the one best-placed to meet it. You may be called to give in an abundant or limited way to it or to draw the need's attention to others more suited to meet it. In some cases you may best serve the need by becoming the rallying point to raise awareness about it, and canvass for resources from others to meet it. In other instances, you may also be called to pray about it but do nothing practical about it in the immediate future. God may sometimes lead one to give substantially to meet a certain need and give little or nothing to another. As a result, an important key to being an effective kingdom steward is keeping our ears tuned to the Spirit's usually quiet voice and gentle promptings; He is the one who best knows how to direct our giving in every instance. This understanding also applies to every area of giving that is not material.

Should we expect a reward for giving?

Some teach that we should give without ever expecting any reward or blessing from God in return. This however, is not the testimony of the scriptures because they tell us time and time again that there is a harvest for faithful givers to the kingdom. We have seen that there is an encouraging expectation of harvest for generous givers from Paul's exhortation on sowing in the previous chapter.

At the other extreme, some today emphasise that giving should always be aimed at receiving specific things from God. The people who promote this viewpoint always ask God's people to *'tag'* or *'command'* virtually every offering based on what they expect God to do in return. Some further claim you have to sow a seed, usually money or other material things, for almost everything you are expecting to receive from God. Again, this is a harmful distortion of biblical teaching about the way God bestows His blessings. He loves us unconditionally and is generous enough to give us all things to freely enjoy without asking for payment in advance or in return as 1Timothy 6:17 testifies. Romans 8:32 also says:

> *He who did not spare his own Son, but gave him up for us all*—**how will he not also, along with him, graciously give us all things?**

These truths should teach us that we do not have to pay up in advance or barter with God in order to receive from Him. They should also encourage us that whatever we *'give'* or *'lose'* in serving God and His kingdom is always a net profit in His divine economy. We do gain in uncountable non-material ways by being a channel of God's giving grace.

Paul also draws our attention to the fact that Saints who give faithfully by 'dispersing', and who bless the poor in particular, gain a righteousness that endures beyond this temporal realm.

'Sowing up'

There is a tendency for some Christians to draw too strong a distinction between what they *'give to God'* (i.e. put in an offering), and what they directly *'give to the poor and needy'* around them. Such a strong distinction is not necessarily backed by the Holy Scriptures. They actually indicate that giving to the poor is equivalent to giving to God Himself:

> Whoever is kind to the poor lends to the LORD,
> and he will reward them for what they have done.
>
> Proverbs 19:17

Also, some would rather give to those they consider their spiritual superiors, and who may be already well-to-do, rather than to their needy counterparts. This is because they have been wrongly taught to deliberately *'sow-up'* and *into* *'good ground'* by giving to apparently 'more blessed' leaders. This is to ensure that they secure ample superior blessings in return. This practice robs a lot of God's lowly people of the provision that should have been given to them through their fellow believers. It also exposes the distorted and unscriptural motives of those who avoid 'sowing-down' by giving to the lowly. Their discriminatory attitude unfortunately causes them to focuses mainly on the expected

97

returns for their giving, rather than on the benefits that would accrue to needy receivers and to God's kingdom.

Givers need to realise that whether they are giving to a prominent ministry or leader, or to a small ministry or humble believer, what matters is to be led by God's Spirit to meet real needs. No believer will lose his reward simply because of the spiritual or economic status of the person or ministry to which they give in obedience to the prompt of Christ's Spirit. As we have already established in our discussion of Principle 2, we are responsible for taking care of church leaders. We should not however neglect non-prominent believers in doing so for selfish reasons. Love for God, His kingdom and people should always be our primary motivation for giving rather than the expectations of blessings and rewards.

Principle Challenge:
Do you readily acknowledge that you simply cannot 'outgive' God whatever the type and amount of resources you give?

Principle Prayer:
Lord, thanks for being faithful to reward my giving. Help me to focus on, and be motivated by, the benefits accruing to Your people and kingdom instead of focusing on selfish gain. Amen.

Principle 7

Giving's reward is more than material

As it is written:
"They have freely scattered their gifts to the poor;
their righteousness endures forever."

2 Corinthians 9:9 (NIV)

The righteous giver

In the scripture above, Paul quotes Psalm 112:9 about a truly righteous man who is committed to relieving the poor by giving generously to meet their needs. Reading the whole of Psalm 112, it is clear that the Psalmist believes that God is committed to blessing those who *'scatter their gifts'* by giving to the poor.

Paul also points out that a major benefit of giving is not material, but an increase in the *'harvest of righteousness'* (2 Corinthians 9:10). This harvest comes by doing what is right, like giving generously to the needy, and is based on a right relationship with God. It is a righteousness that endures forever as the 2 Corinthians 9:9 verse above states. Material blessings only endure for time, but the righteousness bestowed from heaven endures for eternity.

This truth exposes as a lie, one of the worst distortions of the gospel message that has existed from apostolic time. It is that God is obliged to bless us materially if we give in accordance to a particular formula. This enticement is communicated in different permutations of *'sow and be guaranteed to reap bountifully'* teachings. It also comes in the form of fantastic promises such as that of a *'hundred-fold return'* for gifts given.

A true understanding of the verse about the sower's enduring righteousness will make you realise that it is God's will that you be "enriched in all things" – spirit, soul and body – in accordance with your needs. This enrichment puts you in a better position to support kingdom people and causes in the future. God sometimes blesses us beyond our needs by giving us some of our wants because He is generous in nature; He gives to us in more ways than we can ever materially account for. We cannot ultimately lose when we answer His call to sacrifice our material resources in order to bless His people and kingdom. Answering this call releases us to be positioned to receive blessings that money cannot buy. A big part of that is receiving the freedom to love and to serve God without being held back by the love of material things. Other benefits of helping the poor mentioned in Psalm 41:1-3 are deliverance from trouble, protection from enemies and divine healing.

The rich young ruler who came to Jesus in Mathew 19:16-22, discovered in his own case, that undue attachment to material things can prevent one from receiving true heavenly riches. His attachment to riches meant that he was literally stopped from committing to following Jesus. It is ironic that when we freely give Him the 'little' He asks from the much He has richly blessed us with, in His faithfulness, He turns around and blesses us with more than we can ever deserve!

Giving is beyond the material

The point has been made earlier that a lot of us tend automatically to think in terms of material things or money when giving is mentioned. We therefore need a wider understanding of biblical stewardship that expands into other important areas of giving that we need to focus on. Jesus helps to expand our understanding by His teaching about heaven and the reward awaiting His faithful saints there in Mathew 25:31-40:

> *31 "When the Son of Man comes in his glory, and all the angels with him, he will sit on his glorious throne. 32 All the nations will be gathered before him, and he will separate the people one from another as a shepherd separates the sheep from the goats. 33 He will put the sheep on his right and the goats on his left.*
>
> *34 "Then the King will say to those on his right, 'Come, you who are blessed by my Father; take your inheritance, the kingdom prepared for you since the creation of the world. 35 For **I was hungry and you gave me something to eat, I was thirsty and you gave me something to drink, I was a stranger and you invited me in, 36 I needed clothes and you clothed me, I was***

sick and you looked after me, I was in prison and you came to visit me.'

37 "Then the righteous will answer him, 'Lord, when did we see you hungry and feed you, or thirsty and give you something to drink? 38 When did we see you a stranger and invite you in, or needing clothes and clothe you? 39 When did we see you sick or in prison and go to visit you?'

*40 "The King will reply, **'Truly I tell you, whatever you did for one of the least of these brothers and sisters of mine, you did for me.'***

From the words of Jesus above, there are two major lessons to be learned:

The first is that Jesus has a wonderfully expansive view of stewardship that includes providing food, water, lodging, treatment, clothing and visitation to the needy. It is remarkable that most of these provisions are not directly monetary, although some of them may be facilitated with a bit of money. Providing them has more to do with showing practical care and compassion for the needy than merely throwing some spare change in their direction. It means we often have to put on a servant's apron and practically serve those who may never be able to repay us in kind.

The second lesson is that our reward in heaven will be determined, at least in part, by how responsive we are to the practical needs of people we meet throughout our journey on earth. This is true whether or not we are consciously aware of meeting, or failing to meet, their needs.

These words of Jesus further refute the false teaching that we need always to be strategic and deliberate in our giving in order to secure immediate and maximum rewards in this world. It also shows up the lie that believers should always seek to 'sow-up' to people they consider superior to them in order to draw down bigger blessings.

True prosperity

God constantly evaluates how much He can trust us to give liberally to kingdom needs, both now and in the future. He knows if we are holding His resources as faithful stewards or if the resources are holding us as unfaithful ones. He does not want us prospering materially at the expense of our souls. As John prays:

> *Beloved, I pray that you may prosper in all things and be in health, just as your soul prospers.*
> 3 John 2 (New King James Version)

The implication of the above scripture is that no matter how much material stuff a Christian acquires, he is not really living the abundant life that Christ died to give him if he is not prospering in his soul. Soul-prosperity results from an on-going yielding of a believer's will, intellect and emotions to the loving dominion of the Lord. This true prosperity leads to a life that not only abides in Christ, but grows in intimacy and power with Him. It is a life that is, in the immortal words of Paul:

"..taking hold of life that is truly life"- 1 *Timothy 6:19b*
As Jesus warned in Luke 12:15:

> **"Watch out! Be on your guard against all kinds of greed; a man's life does not consist in the abundance of his possessions".**

These and other related scriptures testify that undue focus on physical and material blessings leads to the neglect of the inner life that matters most to God – and should to us. This wrong focus on material things results in the exchange of the true riches of God in Christ for abject spiritual poverty. This is true, even when those who make this exchange gain the glittering goods of this present age in the process. This is because the blinkered pursuit of material things often leads to a lifestyle, not just of spiritual indifference, but one of active sinful compromise as Paul states in 1Timothy 6:10:

For the love of money is a root of all kinds of evil. Some people, eager for money, have wandered from the faith and pierced themselves with many griefs.

Perhaps no other scripture illustrates this truth more than the risen Christ's rebuke of the materially prosperous but spiritually lukewarm Laodicean church in Revelation 3:15-19:

*15 I know your deeds, that you are neither cold nor hot. I wish you were either one or the other! 16 So, because you are lukewarm—neither hot nor cold—I am about to spit you out of my mouth. 17 **You say, 'I am rich; I have acquired wealth and do not need a thing.' But you do not realize that you are wretched, pitiful, poor, blind and naked.** 18 I counsel you to buy from me gold refined in the fire, so you can become rich; and white clothes to wear, so you can cover your shameful nakedness; and salve to put on your eyes, so you can see.19 Those whom I love I rebuke and discipline. So be earnest and repent.*

We need to heed the clear warning contained in the above scripture so we do not fall into the temptation of measuring God's approval of us by how much material blessing we seem to have or acquire. The opposite may actually be the case as we can clearly see in Jesus' unsparing evaluation of the Laodiceans. They were patting themselves on the back for having apparently prospered by the world's standards even though they had become indifferent to what really mattered to their Lord. It is apparent from the record of the devil's second temptation of Jesus in Luke 4:5-8 that it may be possible for a Christian to exchange God's glory and purpose in his life for the attractive material goods of this age. The implication of this is that some apparent 'blessings' actually come from the devil and not from God – and that may be at the expense of one's soul!

Special benefits of faithful giving

In contrast to the Laodiceans' wretched spiritual condition revealed above, a life dedicated to loving service and faithful stewardship of material resources has a number of enriching benefits. Here are some of those that cannot be adequately measured in silver and gold terms:

1. Spiritual freedom: The Lord uses our consistent and faithful giving to free us from the harmful hold of materialism and its associated selfishness. This is always threatening to grab hold of us in order to keep us from following Him wholeheartedly. When we are dedicated to storing our riches in heaven by investing in His kingdom here on earth, our affections are inevitably drawn to heavenly things. It is an inescapable spiritual law that the flow of your life will be to where a substantial part of your time, effort and money are being consistently spent. This is clearly stated in the words of Jesus recorded in Mathew 6:21:

> *For where your treasure is, there your heart will be also.*

A missionary being interviewed on the radio once said: *"From my experience, I have found that the most faithful supporters and intercessors for my ministry are the people who regularly give to support me financially on the mission field. People who promise to pray and keep in touch, but do not give financially often fail to follow-through on their promise. This is because their treasures are not invested in the foreign fields for which they would love to faithfully intercede."*

2. Active kingdom participation: Regular and generous giving helps to transform us from passive receivers of God's blessings to active participants in the advancement of God's Kingdom. This is true even when we are not physically present to carry out the ministry ourselves but enable others to do so by funding them. The testimony of Paul about the missions-supporting Philippian church in Philippians 4:14-18 supports this truth.

3. Better resources management: Generous giving makes us better managers of our resources, particularly when we do so faithfully on a regular basis. This is because we often have to make do with less for ourselves after giving a significant percentage of our income to God and His people. We are therefore better motivated to manage the rest of the income more prudently and efficiently since we have less room for waste and frivolity.

4. Stronger faith: Giving builds up our faith in God because we see Him coming through for us time and time again after giving sacrificially to people and to causes to which He draws our hearts. Even though we may be materially poorer for giving, we often find that God, in His creative benevolence, finds ways to meet our needs and more besides.

We also have the privilege of seeing our faith strengthened by seeing Him do amazing things through the ministries we enable and the people we support by our giving.

5. Uplifting peace and joy: Giving promotes peace and joy in ways that are surprisingly uplifting. Stingy people who hoard their resources rather than use them to bless others are often miserable and are closed in their experience of life. People who receive the gifts also break out in spontaneous thanksgiving and prayers, so the joy is shared between givers and receivers.

6. Eternal dividends: Faithful giving ensures we are making our investments in a place where we cannot lose them – in Heaven! We can look forward to enjoying abundant eternal dividends in the life to come. Believers who give faithfully benefit greatly from storing their treasures in heaven as the words Jesus said in Mathew 6:19-21:

> 19 *"Do not store up for yourselves treasures on earth, where moths and vermin destroy, and where thieves break in and steal.* 20 **But store up for yourselves treasures in heaven, where moths and vermin do not destroy, and where thieves do not break in and steal.** 21 *For where your treasure is, there your heart will be also.*

7. Thanksgiving and intercession: As we will be seeing later in Chapter 9, faithful giving provokes an outbreak of genuine intercession for us. It also inspires thanksgiving to both us and God, who is the ultimate source of every true blessing we are able to share with people.

The most important givers

Church and ministry leaders sometimes get confused about who the major supporters of their work really are because of the pressure they face to secure funding for it. It should be acknowledged that people who contribute most significantly to advancing God's kingdom are the people who freely dedicate their time, talents and treasures to serving their churches and ministries. This is true, even if the amount of money they give may be relatively small due to their limited means. They are often the ones growing most in the love and grace of Christ. They are in the cutting edge of ministry; His arms and legs to practically do the work. These believers are not inferior to the occasional rich donors who usually have little or no practical input into actual ministry, and should not be treated as such. If care is not taken, organisations who fail to understand this reality may fall into the dangerous trap of being hijacked by people who have money to give but whose agenda is not necessarily Christ's. It may be wise to rely more on the 'small' gifts of a number of faithful Christians rather than on big ones rich individual or corporate donors.

While it is not wrong to be rich and to give large amounts to charities and ministries, it is important that such gifts are outflows of a life dedicated to the Lord himself.

There is definitely a rich supply of spiritual life and grace flowing to people who commit the totality of their lives to serving the kingdom. They are supernaturally enabled to grasp life that is life indeed and to enjoy the true riches of Christ as they grow in His grace. These are the people who are truly *"enriched in every way"* to make the greatest impact for God's kingdom.

Principle Challenge: `
How readily and regularly do you focus on the intangible long-term benefits of giving instead of looking for immediate material rewards?

Principle Prayer:
Lord, please open my eyes to see the limitless rewards of giving. Help me to see way beyond material rewards that are quick to attract me but are ultimately of secondary importance. Amen.

Principle 8

Balance sowing with eating

10 Now he who supplies seed to the sower and bread for food will also supply and increase your store of seed and will enlarge the harvest of your righteousness. 11 You will be enriched in every way so that you can be generous on every occasion, and through us your generosity will result in thanksgiving to God.

2 Corinthians 9:10-11 (NIV)

Eating and sowing

Using an analogy that was no doubt familiar to the readers of his day, who lived in a largely agricultural agrarian society, Paul explains that God gives us both bread for eating (what to consume for our own needs and even some of our wants) and seed for sowing (what should be given for kingdom purposes) . Our responsibility as faithful stewards is therefore to constantly seek Him for wisdom to discern between what to eat and what to sow.

As we have established earlier, on one hand God gives us all things for our rich enjoyment. So He wants us to enjoy His provisions without guilt. Paul sums this truth up brilliantly when he urged Timothy to admonish the rich in 1Timothy 6:17:

*Command those who are rich in this present world not to be arrogant nor to put their hope in wealth, which is so uncertain, but to put their hope in **God, who richly provides us with everything for our enjoyment.***

On the other hand, God wants us to be generous in distributing what He gives us. This is a more responsible, joyful and fulfilling way of living than just spending or keeping most of His blessings for ourselves. The challenge we have therefore is to consistently keep these seemingly opposing practices of eating and sowing in proper tension. As Paul further says in 1Timothy 6:18-19:

*18 Command them to do good, to **be rich in good deeds, and to be generous and willing to share.** 19 In this way they will lay up treasure for themselves as a firm foundation for the coming age, so that they may take hold of the life that is truly life.*

Being *'generous and willing to share'* is the disposition of heart that separates a grace-filled person from one who is tight-fisted with his or her worldly goods.

Responsible giving

It is important to maintain a proper balance between consuming what God gives us and giving an appropriate portion of it to kingdom purposes. Doing both is not necessarily as contradictory as it may initially seem. They are actually both necessary for joyful and fruitful Christian living. Failure to do both spoils our enjoyment of what God freely gives us on one side. On the other, selfish withholding and spending prevents us from meeting kingdom needs adequately.

Establishing this dynamic balance is what makes us effective, joy-filled stewards of our gracious Master. There is however no certain formula for achieving the balance at all times. Every believer is called to continually assess what he has in line with the needs around him in order to decide how best to distribute his resources. A helpful way to do this is by considering the major areas and boundaries of stewardship discussed earlier under Principle 2. This may then form the basis of prayerfully budgeting what is to be given or consumed regularly and occasionally.

Duly withholding

It is important not to yield to feelings of false guilt or give in to pressure when we cannot give at all , or as much as requested to a particular need being presented. Sometimes, the reason you will not give as much or at all may be because you have good reasons not to. A scripture that, surprisingly, may help one to understand this truth best is found in the book of Proverbs. Ironically, it is one which is used almost exclusively to encourage people to give liberally. It nevertheless contains a highly relevant nugget of truth about the balance between giving and keeping. It reads thus:

> *One person gives freely, yet gains even more;*
> *another **withholds unduly**, but comes to poverty.*

Proverbs 11:24

From the emphasised part of the above scripture, it can be deduced that even in the place of generous giving, it is appropriate to withhold enough for personal needs and family responsibilities. The admonition here is therefore to encourage generosity by not withholding more than is right, while realising it is appropriate to withhold; as much as it is right. What we duly 'withhold' may then be saved, invested or used to meet other needs as the Spirit leads us.

The key to balance

As was discussed in the introductory chapter, a major key to understanding this balance is realising that we do not really own anything ourselves. Rather, we are kingdom stewards entrusted by God with resources of time, talents and treasures that we are to use, enjoy and distribute as our Master leads daily.

Most of us regularly fall into the temptation of thinking: *"A percentage – usually the tithe plus a bit more as offering – of what I have or make belongs to the Lord and must be given to Him. I may then go on and spend the rest as I like without recourse to*

Him". This kind of thinking is based on the false premise that we own anything ourselves in the first instance. It fails to acknowledge that all we have is kept in our care by Him. It also makes it easier for us to wrongfully divide our lives into separate *'spiritual'* and *'secular'* zones. The attitude leads to us making decisions about the use of our resources that contradict God's purpose for us in particular, and for His kingdom in general. These errors ultimately lead us to become unfaithful, or at best only partially effective stewards of His grace.

David, though an Old Testament Saint, had a more wholesome understanding of the one who really owns what we have. He reveals this understanding in 1 Chronicles 29:14:

> *"But who am I, and who are my people, that we should be able to give as generously as this?* **Everything comes from you, and we have given you only what comes from your hand.**

If you read the entire chapter from which the above scripture was extracted, it is clear that David and his leadership were intentionally careful to generously provide for the temple from their personal wealth. Yet, David made light of their sacrifice by saying that what they gave was not theirs but God's in the first place! God, who is the real owner of 'our' resources, therefore reserves the right to direct us on how best to deploy them for the benefit of His kingdom. Discovering He delights in guiding us about how best to use, give or withhold them from time to time should really encourage us.

We will not do much wrong if we ensure our giving reflects the important areas of concerns highlighted in the discussion of the original purpose of tithing in Chapter 4. We should do this in conjunction with the others discussed in the main areas of giving in the Chapter 2. God certainly wants us to be richer in our understanding and experience of giving than most of us are now. So if we are willing, He is able to lead us into an adventure of more profitable and fulfilling stewardship of the resources He places in our care.

Principle Challenge:
How properly do you balance the eating and the sowing of your God-given resources?

Principle Prayer:
Lord, help me to learn to balance the conflicting demands of eating and sowing in a way that truly blesses others, enriches me and glorifies You. Help me to always seek and receive Your wisdom continually in this area. Amen.

Principle 9

Giving inspires thanksgiving and intercession

12 This service that you perform is not only supplying the needs of the Lord's people but is also overflowing in many expressions of thanks to God. 13 Because of the service by which you have proved yourselves, others will praise God for the obedience that accompanies your confession of the gospel of Christ, and for your generosity in sharing with them and with everyone else. 14 And in their prayers for you their hearts will go out to you, because of the surpassing grace God has given you.

2 Corinthians 9:12-14 (NIV)

Inspired thanksgiving and intercession

When we lovingly give to others and to worthy causes, the usual result is that heartfelt appreciation comes to us in return. Praises and thanksgiving also rise up to God who is the ultimate source of the gifts we give. Individual saints and ministries need to realise more than ever, that their most fervently faithful supporters and intercessors will often be those who have been blessed by their benevolence and ministry. This secret is one of the fundamental truths in the words of Jesus quoted by Paul in Acts 20:35:

*In everything I did, I showed you that by this kind of hard work we must help the weak, remembering the words the Lord Jesus himself said: '**It is more blessed to give than to receive.**' "*

One of the outstanding blessings of giving is that it inspires the receivers to spontaneously pray for many blessings – often in excess of the material gift – upon the giver's life. God delights in answering such heart-felt prayers and He is always more generous in His answers than we were in our giving. The flip-side of this truth is that receivers should not neglect to be thankful to and pray for the people used to bless them. This is what sustains the cycle of divine blessing for all givers and receivers through the ages. Christian leaders would therefore do well to regularly thank and proclaim blessings upon those they lead for giving their resources to the causes of the kingdom they champion.

Giving is proof of obedience

From the 2 Corinthians 9:13 text above, Paul clearly makes the point that your stewardship of material resources shown by your giving is a vital measure of the level of the "obedience of your confession of Christ". Claiming to be obedient to the gospel of Christ without giving faithfully to support it is therefore contradictory. James, when speaking about the practical outworking of the faith by giving to needy Christians, puts it starkly:

118

*14 What good is it, my brothers and sisters, if someone claims to have faith but has no deeds? Can such faith save them? 15 Suppose a brother or a sister is without clothes and daily food. 16 If one of you says to them, "Go in peace; keep warm and well fed," but does nothing about their physical needs, what good is it? 17 **In the same way, faith by itself, if it is not accompanied by action, is dead.***

James 2:14-17

Amy Carmichael, the Irish Presbyterian missionary who gave her life to selflessly serving the poor people of India summarises the above truths thus: *"One can give without loving, but one cannot love without giving".*

Principle Challenge:
How faithfully do you thank God for the blessings you have received from others and intercede for them?

Principle Prayer:
Lord, thank You for the incredible thanksgiving and intercession that giving inspires. I pray You will use me more than ever to facilitate these. Amen.

Principle 10

God is the greatest giver

15 Thanks be to God for His indescribable gift!
2 Corinthians 9:15, NIV)

Highest level of giving

We must acknowledge that irrespective of how often and how much we give, our sacrifice will always pale in comparison with the matchless and indescribable gift that God gave us in Christ! Jesus Himself puts it brilliantly when He said to Nicodemus:

> **For God so loved the world that he gave his one and only Son**, *that whoever believes in him shall not perish but have eternal life.*
>
> John 3:16

'John the Beloved' summarises the truth in these words of Jesus when he reminds us in 1 John 4:19:

We love because he first loved us

Regularly meditating on these simple but powerful words should keep us humble about the discharge of our stewardship duties. A major key to giving ourselves, and by extension our material goods, freely and fully to God is the gaining of the clear realisation of how much Christ Himself sacrificed in order to give us eternal life. It is from this boundless love and life that all other spiritual and material blessings that we receive flow. Perhaps no human words may be found to sufficiently express the extent of His sacrifice than those of Paul in Philippians 2:5-8:

> 5 In your relationships with one another, have the same mind-set as Christ Jesus:
> 6 Who, being in very nature God,
> did not consider equality with God something to be used to his own advantage;
> 7 **rather, he made himself nothing**
> **by taking the very nature of a servant**,
> being made in human likeness.
> 8 And being found in appearance as a man,
> **he humbled himself**
> **by becoming obedient to death** —
> even death on a cross!

Giving is a privilege

All our giving, service and sacrifice must be done with an 'attitude of gratitude' to the God who has blessed us with the life and resources we give in the first place. It is He who has counted us worthy of being in a position to use those resources to bless His kingdom and people. We should adopt the same mind-set the Apostles had when they sacrificed and suffered for the gospel in the face of persecution:

> *40 His speech persuaded them.* **They called the apostles in and had them flogged. Then they ordered them not to speak in the name of Jesus, and let them go.**
> *41 The apostles left the Sanhedrin,* **rejoicing because they had been counted worthy of suffering disgrace for the Name.** *42 Day after day, in the temple courts and from house to house, they never stopped teaching and proclaiming the good news that Jesus is the Messiah.*
>
> *Acts 5: 40-42*

We, like them, should count it a privilege to serve His people and kingdom with our life and means, no matter how much it costs us. This will help us to continue serving and giving even when it is costly to do so. We serve a God who is committed to blessing us with all spiritual blessings in the heavenly places as well as meeting our material needs here on earth. We cannot do better than to follow the example of Jesus who says:

> **"…it is more blessed to give than to receive"** – Acts 20:35b

It is definitely beneficial to receive from others but such blessings are somewhat 'limited' no matter the quantity and quality of what we may receive. This is because, although receiving is good, the 'more blessed' way is actually to give to others rather than receiving from them. This truth may not make sense when viewed from the world's perspective as it counts receiving as profit and giving as loss. Receiving is often based on the humble acknowledgement of our need, while giving is based on the faithful acknowledgement of our responsibility to share the blessing we already have. Both of these are needed in balance if we are to live fruitful lives. When giving is done in love and obedience, it has benefits that far outstrip what we give. So those who wish to live in the realms of potentially unlimited blessings need to commit themselves to using every opportunity they have to be a blessing to others. We should particularly prioritise being a blessing to God's people and kingdom first as Paul encourages us to do in Galatians 6:10 and Mathew 6:33.

Principle Challenge:
Do you freely acknowledge that all that you or anyone else can give pales in comparison with God's matchless gift of Christ?

Principle Prayer:
God, thank You for Your indescribable gift of Christ to me. Help me to be continually inspired by Your boundless love and the matchless grace of Christ in my stewardship.

Last Words

Giving is a love relationship with the Master

It is my fervent prayer and hope that you have not just read but diligently engaged with the principles we have discussed in this book. I hope this is true , even if you may not fully agree with some of the points made. I believe this fresh engagement has brought you to a greater realisation that giving is not just about parting with some of your worldly goods for a good cause or worthy person, noble as these are. Rather, it is about managing the resources of a loving and benevolent Master who fully owns us and all that we have. Consequently, giving has more to do with your open heart of love for the Master and His Kingdom than the size of your wallet and its openness towards others.

I trust you are now more resolutely persuaded that your acceptability before God is based on the finished work of Christ on our behalf, rather than on your performance of giving and service, as important as those may be. It is true that our service and giving go a long way in determining our reward in both time and eternity. Nevertheless, our greatest joy and confidence should be that we are assured of a place in the Father's house as illustrated in Jesus' admonition to the disciples in Luke 10: 1-20. He had sent them out on a ministry expedition and they came back beaming with joy as they recounted the wonderful exploits they had done in His name. In response, He firmly redirected the focus of their joy to the security of their relationship with the heavenly Father, shifting it away from what they had accomplished on the mission field in His name. In line with that admonition, our own fulfilment and joy should be based primarily, not on our performance or lack thereof, but on our relationship with Him.

We must resolutely refuse to yield to the temptation of divorcing how we live our lives daily from what we give materially to God and His people. It is the condition of the altar of our hearts that makes our giving acceptable to God and not the other way round. Jesus confirms this truth when He rebuked the Pharisees and the Teachers of the Law for their hypocrisy in Mathew 23:16-22. Gifts that do not come from a righteous lifestyle are unlikely to be acceptable to God. Even in the Old Testament, God warned that the lifestyle of His people determines the acceptability of their gifts to Him:

> *You must not bring the earnings of a female prostitute or of a male prostitute into the house of the LORD your God to pay any vow, because the LORD your God detests them both.*
> Deuteronomy 23:18

It therefore follows that professing Christians who cheat, steal or prostitute themselves to get material things deceive themselves if they think that they can make themselves and their money acceptable by tithing and giving offerings from such incomes.

The import of the above is that faithful and fruitful giving actually flows from a healthy, living relationship with the Master who created us for, and longs to have an on-going loving fellowship with us. It is in the context of this love-walk with, and obedience to, Him that He inspires and directs our giving. He does this in a way that best serves the needs of individuals, churches and ministries with whom we come in contact as we listen to Him. The more we commit to being eager and loving listeners to His gentle voice, the better able we are to direct our giving to His glory. A life of commitment to the joys and discipline of daily personal devotion is essential if this is to continue.

It is hoped that you have now seen that giving goes beyond just meeting immediate needs to providing for God's people and his work in the future. Doing this practically means being alert for the opportunities we get to support worthy people, causes and ministries in the middle to long term. I was reminded about this truth recently when someone close to me received a 'Save our soul' message from a Christian family who were in great need far away in the third world. The wife was pregnant and in need of some money for medical treatment. The money they immediately needed was relatively small and could be easily provided by him. However, after thinking and praying about their wider needs, he was moved to give them multiples of what they requested. He did this in order to help infuse life into their small business that was suffering as a result of their lack of funds. The giver confessed that he did not immediately think of giving that much even though it was obvious from the outset that their need ran deeper than the original request. He was able to give them long-term sustenance due to a combination of understanding the principles we have been sharing, and seeking God's heart about their plight. Even though the 'sacrifice' he made was greater than initially planned, it was more than worth it as he heard their testimony and thanksgiving for the abundant provision.

The flipside of the above example is that we should also be free not to give at all, or only give in a limited way to an apparent need or request. This is because our circumstances may not permit us to meet the need at that particular time or the Spirit may restrain us from doing so. This is more reason why we need to constantly listen to the Holy Spirit's guidance about what or what not to give.

As an example, someone close to me used to feel terrible about saying no to most requests made to him. As a result, he has put his family in financial trouble as he tried to meet too many expectations in the past. He actually still struggles with this challenge from time to time, particularly when he sees what he considers to be a genuine need. Thankfully, his wife has often been the voice of reason and has helped him balance his giving with his other responsibilities. My experience of talking with other couples has shown a similar balancing act, albeit with some role reversals. Learning when to say 'No' or 'Yes, but only so much' to a request is actually a sign of discernment resulting from spiritual maturity.

Hence, we must resist the temptation to allow ourselves to be guilt-tripped or manipulated into giving inappropriately.

As you continue your journey of stewardship, I pray that you will continue to actively practice these principles so that you can be freed from all legalistic, inflexible and spiritually unproductive attitudes to giving. I pray you will become much more fruitful and effective in serving the Master with all you are and have. Please keep these words of Paul in mind:

> *"it is God who works in you to will and to act in order to fulfil his good purpose."*
>
> Philippians 2:13

Be encouraged that God appreciates all that you have given , and are still giving , because of your love for Him and for His precious people. He appreciates your heart for His kingdom and your obedience to His inspiration in the managing of your stewardship in all areas of life. He can be counted faithful to reward you generously in this world and the next!

Final Challenge:
How well do you relate your giving to your relationship with God and the way you live your life from day to day?

Final Prayer:
Lord, help me to appreciate more meaningfully, how my giving relates to my walk of faith and love for You. Help me

to overcome the temptation of divorcing my material giving from my daily relationship with You. Amen.

About the Book

Have you ever wondered why the subjects of giving and material stewardship cause so much controversy in the Church? Do you ever struggle with questions like: To whom should I give? How much should I give? How should I give? and For what reasons should I give? If so, this book is for you. It explores what the Bible, particularly the New Testament, teaches about Christian giving from a stewardship perspective. It examines in some detail, how the Apostle Paul used the example of the loving and sacrificial giving of Jesus, and that of the Macedonian church, to encourage the Corinthian church in their stewardship challenge. Paul's encouraging appeal forms the basis from which ten principles of stewardship are derived and discussed. Understanding and living by these principles are as relevant and as helpful to us today as they were to the first Church community. Committing to them should hopefully help you rise up to greater faithfulness and more fruitful stewardship.

About the Author

Funsho Oluro is a gifted minister who has been called to teach, encourage and equip the saints in their journey to greater spiritual maturity and effectiveness in life and ministry. He has more than two decades experience of doing this in various interdenominational and international contexts. He is a 'tent-making' professional Surveyor who seeks to invest his time and energy into studying, practising and teaching God's powerful and life-transforming word with simplicity and in the power of the Spirit.

He is married to Linda, with whom he has two children and they make their home in London, United Kingdom.

Printed in Great Britain
by Amazon

84327424R00078